LIVING
WITH
QUILTS

Vanessa-Ann's

LIVING
WITH
QUILTS

Meredith® Press
New York, N.Y.

For Meredith® Press:

Director: Elizabeth P. Rice
Product Development Manager: Patricia Van Note
Editorial Project Manager: Maryanne Bannon
Production Manager: Bill Rose

Designers:

Trice Boerens, Margaret Shields Marti, Jo Packham,
Darlene Scow, Ann Seely, Florence Stacey, Joyce
Stewart, Susan Whitelock, Terrece Beesley Woodruff

For The Vanessa-Ann Collection:

Owners: Jo Packham and Terrece Beesley Woodruff

Staff: Ana Ayala, Gloria Baur, Vicki Burke, Sandra
D. Chapman, Tim Fairholm, Susan Jorgensen,
Margaret Shields Marti, Barbara Milburn, Lisa Miles,
Caryol Patterson, Reva Smith Petersen, Pam
Randall, Leslie Rodak, Gayle Voss, Nancy Whitley

Photographers: David Allison,
Ryne Hazen, John McIntosh

*With sincere gratitude for their trust and
cooperation, The Vanessa-Ann Collection
thanks Trends and Traditions and Ivywood
of Ogden, Utah, and The Reston Market
Inn of Reston, Virginia, for allowing us to
photograph at their locations.*

ISBN: 0-696-02344-X
First Printing: 1991
Library of Congress: 89-063582

Published by Meredith® Press

Distributed by Meredith Corporation, Des Moines, Iowa

10 9 8 7 6 5 4 3 2 1

❖ ❖ ❖ ❖ ❖ ❖

For Reva,

Our quilted masterpieces would sit in seclusion if you were not here to orchestrate their debut.

With our respect and appreciation,

Jo and Terrece

❖ ❖ ❖ ❖ ❖ ❖

Dear Quilter,

Throughout the centuries, patchwork quilts have been a part of daily life for many women. Traditionally, efforts were limited to bed and crib quilts. *Living With Quilts* continues the fine tradition of patchwork quilting and applique, but brings the quilt from the bedroom into every area of the home.

Designed by The Vanessa-Ann Collection, *Living With Quilts* presents an array of exciting designs and ideas for creating and decorating with quilts. Within these pages you'll find designs that are based on well-loved traditional designs, as well as new contemporary designs that will soon become classics.

Whatever your quilting skills, you'll discover patterns and easy-to-follow instructions that are accurate and clear. Each project is beautifully photographed in settings that will provide you with a wide range of creative decorating ideas.

We at Meredith Press are dedicated to bringing you craft books with exciting, original designs and clear, precise how-to instructions. We sincerely hope you'll enjoy making the projects featured in *Living With Quilts* and enjoy their beauty in every room of your home!

Sincerely,

Pat Van Note

Pat Van Note
Product Development Manager

Contents

❖   ❖   ❖   ❖   ❖   ❖

music: \myu-zik\ *n* 1a: the science or

art of ordering tones or sounds in

succession, in combination, and in

temporal relationships to produce a

composition having unity and continuity

syn see QUILTING

We at The Vanessa-Ann Collection believe Webster's definition of music is also a very accurate definition of the art of quilt making. In fact, you've probably noticed that for nearly a dozen years our love for quilts has surfaced now and then in our cross-stitch books. So, utilizing a musical metaphor, we have composed a full concert of quilts for you—a score for every style and taste, full of simple passages, powerful phrases and striking sonatas.

Singing to the song of a needle and thread, our designers have worked closely to bring *Living With Quilts* to you. They are the instruments of the orchestra, the members of the choir. Each plays a different part. Combined, the result is a breathtaking composition of visual poetry. Measure by measure, piece by piece, each of our designers uses her own individual talents to create the quilted masterpieces in this book.

For example, Terrece Woodruff begins with the finished pictoral design well in mind, and, using a pencil and ruler, systematically proceeds to break her work of art into geometric components. She designs with colored pencils, carefully testing the values and hues against each other. Then she selects just the right bright, rich fabrics that will bring her melody to life.

In contrast, Trice Boerens begins with a traditional quilting pattern made from some of her favorite fabrics, building and cutting them apart, experimenting with color and texture, until she "is just as surprised as the next person" at the results. Cautioning against too much careful matching in selecting the fabrics for a quilt, Trice tells how she comes upon her unique arrangements. First, she spreads out all of the fabrics in her collection. If she is building blocks in blue, for example, she considers every piece of blue fabric and then removes the ones that are out of tune with each other. Next, she may add all of her orange and yellow fabrics, gradually eliminating the pieces that aren't working, until she's found the new tone and timbre she's seeking.

Then there's Jo Packham, who is truly a virtuoso at Victorian quilting. She is inspired by soft, delicate colors in silks and wools, velvets and rayons. Her pieces resonate with embellishments—buttons, pearls, ribbons and dried flowers. It is Jo who can envision the finished look of each quilted design. Her philosophy reflects the company's: Quilts are to live with, to touch, to use where you least expect them. A room full of quilts is an ensemble of harmony, making it a warmer and friendlier place to live.

So, with *Living With Quilts* as your sheet music, you can now become the maestro. It is our fervent wish that you will be as content and fulfilled as we are with these orchestrations, and that the lyrics you fashion in your quilts will live forever. ❖

Home Is Where the Heart Is

Shades of Love

Layer on layer, pattern on pattern, this quilt offers a comfortable blending of dusty colors that radiate an affectionate ambience.

Finished size: 37" x 37"

Materials:

Scraps of lavender fabric:
  16 of Template A

⅝ yard of mauve-print fabric:
  Four 4½" x 30" border pieces

⅛ yard of a different mauve-print fabric:
  One of Template B
  Eight of Template D

Scraps of a different mauve-print fabric:
  16 of Template A

2 yards of lavender-print fabric:
  One 37" x 37" backing piece
  16 of Template F
  Four of Template A
  Four HEARTs
  4½ yards of 1¼"-wide bias for binding

Scrap of a different lavender-print fabric:
  Eight of Template D

⅛ yard of green-print fabric:
  Four of Template E

¼ yard of blue-print fabric
  16 of Template C
  Four of Template E

¼ yard of gray-print fabric
  16 of Template D

⅜ yard of green fabric:
  Four of Template E
  24 2" x 8" sashing pieces

⅛ yard of light-blue fabric:
  Four 1" x 30" border strips

1⅛ yards of batting:
  One 37" x 37" piece

Pink thread for quilting
One purchased quilting template,
  approximately 6" square

Directions:

1. **Make center block.** Join the four lavender-print As to the corners of the mauve-print B to make the center block (Diagram 1).

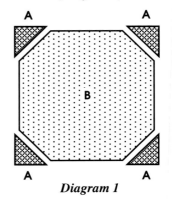

Diagram 1

2. **Make four-corner blocks.** Join four blue-print Cs, four gray-print Ds and one blue-print E to make three rows (Diagram 2). Join the rows to make one four-corner block. Repeat to make four four-corner blocks.

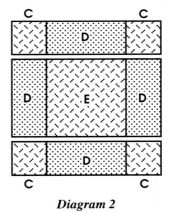

Diagram 2

3. **Make heart blocks.** Join one lavender A to one mauve-print A (Diagram 3). Repeat to make 16 A/A sets.

Diagram 3

Join four A/A sets, two lavender-print Ds, two mauve-print Ds, and one green-print E to make three rows (Diagram 4). Join the rows to make one heart block. Applique one HEART to the center of each green-print E. Repeat to make four heart blocks.

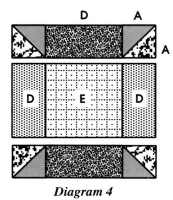

Diagram 4

4. **Complete quilt top.** Join four lavender-print Fs and three 2" x 8" green sashing pieces to make one sashing row (Diagram 5). Repeat to make four sashing rows.

Diagram 5

Join all of the blocks with the remaining 2" x 8" green sashing pieces to make three rows. Then join the rows and the sashing rows (Diagram 6).

Diagram 6

5. **Add border.** Stitch two 1" x 30" light-blue strips to the sides of the quilt top. Trim the ends to fit the quilt. Stitch two 1" x 30" light-blue strips to the top and bottom edges of the quilt (Diagram 7).

Join one green E to each end of a 4½" x 30" mauve-print strip. Repeat to make two sets. Stitch the remaining mauve-print strips to the sides of the quilt top. Then stitch the E/mauve-strip/E sets to the remaining sides of the quilt (Diagram 7).

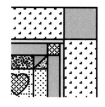

Diagram 7

6. **Mark quilting lines.** Trace the purchased template design in the center of the center block. Mark all green sashing pieces with 1½'-long lines ½" apart. Mark an "X" in each lavender-print F. Mark the lines in the four-corner (Diagram 8) and heart (Diagram 9) blocks. Mark a 1"-wide diamond grid on all mauve-print borders. Trace the heart pattern (without seam allowances) in each green corner E.

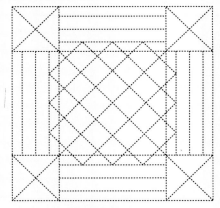

Diagram 8

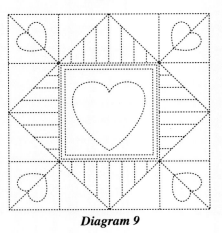

Diagram 9

7. **Complete quilt.** Layer the quilt backing piece (wrong side up), batting, and quilt top. Baste. Using pink thread, quilt all marked lines, all sashing and border seams, and in-the-ditch of each appliqued heart. Bind with lavender-print bias. Miter the corners. ❖

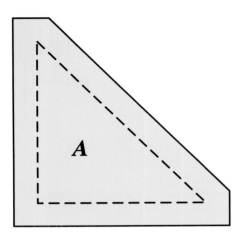

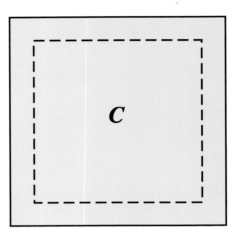

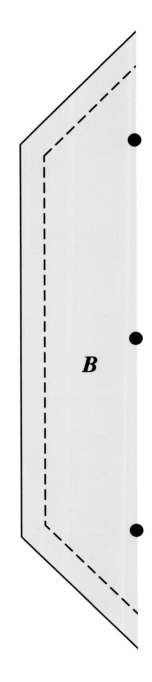

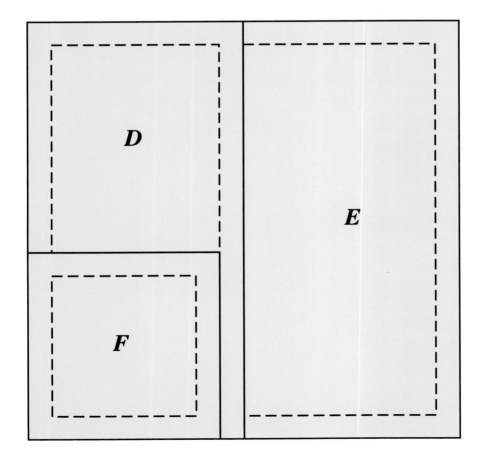

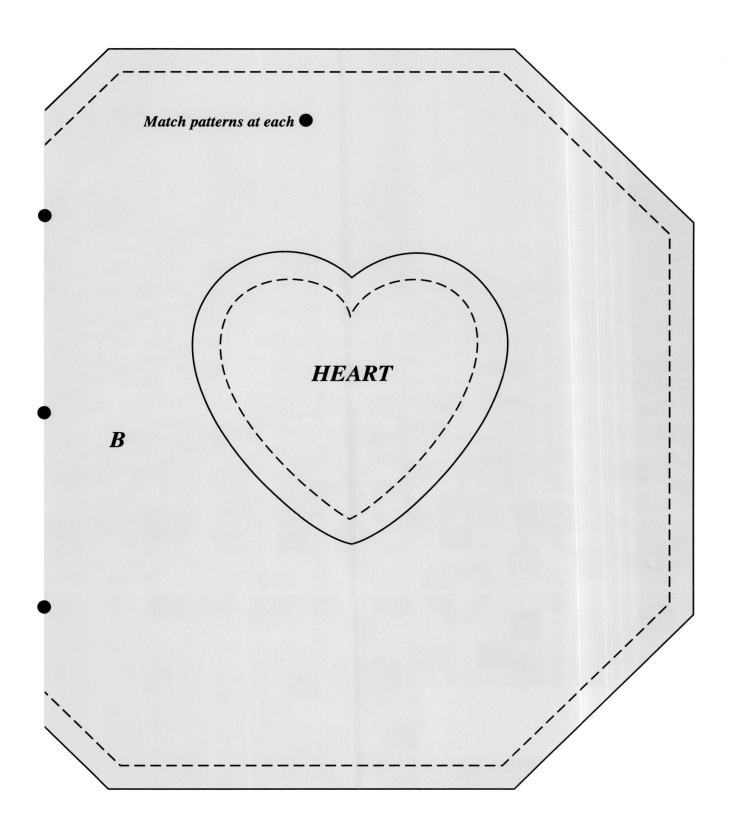

Match patterns at each ●

HEART

B

Sweet Hearts

Directions:

1. **Applique heart blocks.** Applique one HEART to the center of each tan-print A. Repeat to make 49 heart blocks.

2. **Make tan and navy blocks.** Join one tan-print B and one navy-print B on the short edges (Diagram 1). Repeat to make two pairs. Then join the pairs to make a tan/navy-print block. Repeat to make 52 tan/navy blocks.

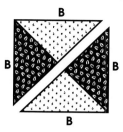

Diagram 1

3. **Make nine-square blocks.** Join nine Cs, each of a different print, to make a nine-square block (Diagram 2). Alternate navy- and red-print Cs with tan-print Cs (see photo). Repeat to make 94 nine-square blocks.

Diagram 2

4. **Piece quilt top.** With all heart points toward the bottom of the quilt, join 15 rows of 13 blocks each, noting the placement of the darker fabrics in the tan/navy blocks (Diagram 3).

Diagram 3

Whoever said "Home is where the heart is" must have envisioned this fetching quilt. It combines the classic colors of tan, navy and red pieced in a bold and distinctive pattern.

Finished size: 87½" x 99½"

Materials:

7 yards of tan-print fabric:
    49 of Template A
    Two 45" x 102" backing pieces

1⅜ yards total of assorted red-print fabrics:
    49 HEARTs

1¾ yards total of assorted navy-print fabrics:
    104 of Template B

1¾ yards total of assorted tan-print fabrics:
    104 of Template B

5 yards of assorted tan-, navy-, and red-print fabrics:
    846 of Template C

2⅝ yards of red-print striped fabric:
    Two 1" x 92" border strips
    Two 1" x 80" border strips
    (The width of each strip is determined by the design in the stripe. All measurements here are based upon a finished width of ½", but the red-print strip in the model is actually ⅜" wide.)

3 yards of navy fabric:
    Two 4¾" x 102" border strips
    Two 4¾" x 90" border strips
    11 yards of 3"-wide bias for binding

One 90" x 102" piece of batting
Cream thread for quilting
Navy thread for quilting

5. **Add border.** Stitch the long edge of one navy border strip to the long edge of one red-print border strip of a corresponding length. Repeat to make two long and two short border strips. Stitch the longer border strips to the right and left edges of the quilt top, matching the centers. Stitch the shorter border strips to the top and bottom edges of the quilt top, matching the centers. Miter the corners.

6. **Mark quilting lines.** Mark the center of each navy border strip. Mark 3" on either side of the center mark, and then at 3½" intervals. Trace the Border Quilting Pattern onto the navy border, repeating the pattern with the point of the triangle on the marks and reversing the pattern at the center (Diagram 4). Also trace the Center Wing Pattern. Repeat on all four border strips. Trace the Corner Quilting Pattern at each corner where the border strips meet.

To mark the diagonal lines on the quilt top, begin on the seams of the tan diamond shape around the center heart. Then continue to mark parallel diamonds; the lines will intersect diagonally through each 1"-square of the nine-square blocks. Do not mark through the hearts (Diagram 5). Mark the entire pieced section of the quilt top.

7. **Complete quilt.** Stitch the two backing pieces together along one 102" edge. Layer the quilt back (wrong side up), batting and the quilt top. Baste. Using cream thread, quilt all marked lines of the pieced quilt top and in-the-ditch around each heart. Then echo quilt ¼" inside each heart. Using navy thread, quilt all marked lines on the border. Bind the quilt with the navy bias. Miter the corners. ❖

Diagram 4

Diagram 5

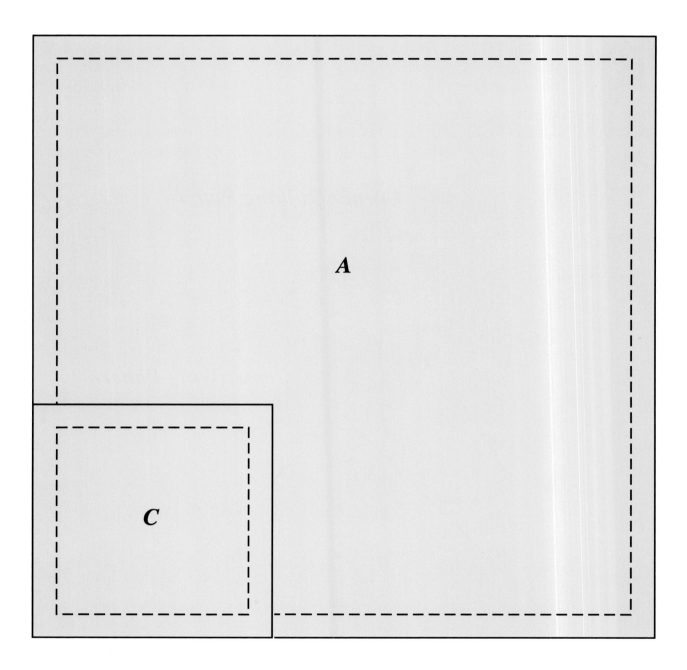

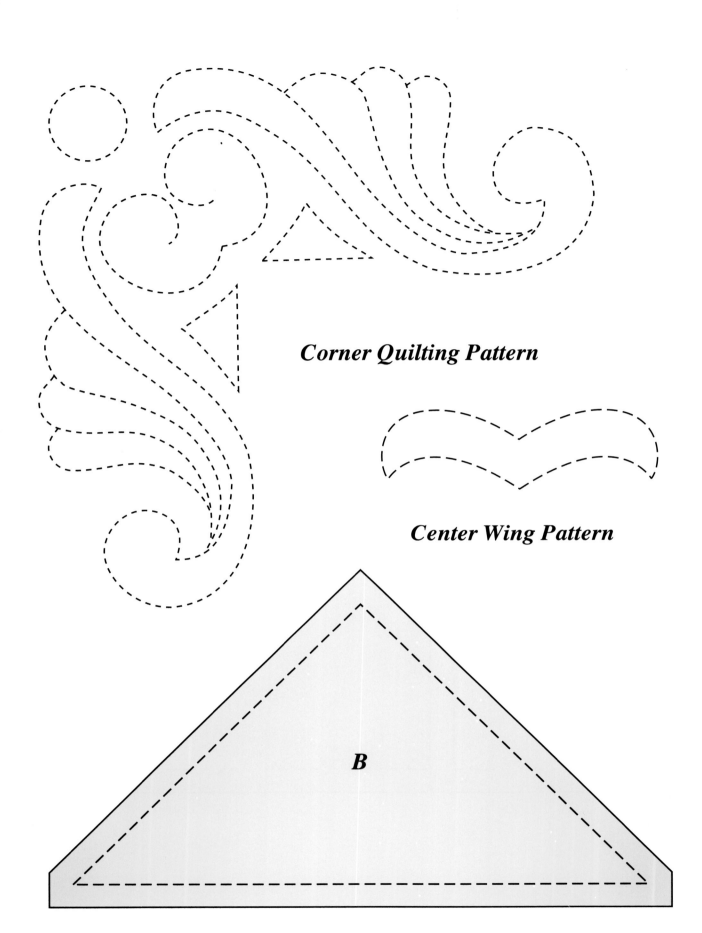

Corner Quilting Pattern

Center Wing Pattern

B

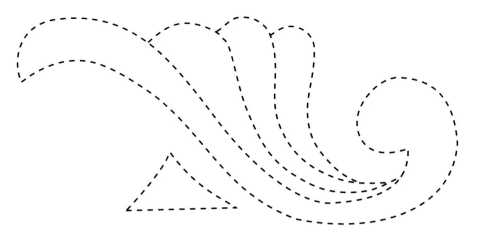

Border Quilting Pattern

HEART

Charming Country Sampler

Have you a flair for fabric? Then this is definitely the quilt for you. Although only sixteen fabrics are listed in the materials section, the model itself uses many more. For example, "navy prints" becomes something of a generic term for the numerous small prints used, each containing navy as the predominant color. Mixing and matching has never been so much fun!

Directions:

1. **Make house block.** Cut the following fabrics:
   One ROOF from red pindot
   One HEART from red pindot
   One of Template A from tan floral
   24 of Template B from assorted prints
   Four of Template C from navy
   Two 1¾" x 1½" pieces from navy-print for chimneys
   Two 2" x 5" pieces from tan print
   One 5" x 1¾" piece from tan print
   Two 1¾" x 4½" pieces from navy plaid
   Two 7½" x 1¾" pieces from navy plaid
   One 2½" x 4½" piece from navy plaid
   Four of Template D from muslin
   Two of Template E from muslin
   One 2" x 5" piece from muslin
   One 1" x 5¼" piece from muslin
   Two 1¾" x 4½" piece from muslin
   Two 7½" x 1" pieces from muslin

Assemble the house; Diagram 1. Then applique the red pindot heart to the house where indicated. Assemble four fans; Diagram 2.

Finished size: 41" x 41"

Materials:

Fabrics:
   2 yards of muslin
   1¼ yards of tan/rose print
   1¼ yards of cream/rose print
   1 yard of navy
   ¼ yard of tan print
   ⅛ yard of red pindot
   ⅛ yard of navy print
   Scraps of tan floral
   Scraps of navy plaid
   Scraps of red/black print
   Scraps of dusty blue print
   Scraps of rose print
   Scraps of red plaid
   Scraps of red/tan print

1¼ yards of polyester fleece
Matching threads for construction
Navy and cream threads for quilting
4¾ yards of small cording

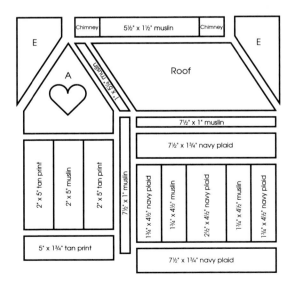

Diagram 1

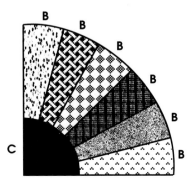

Diagram 2

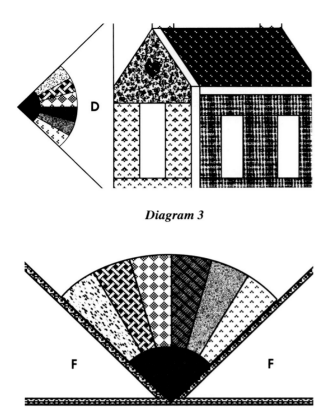

Diagram 3

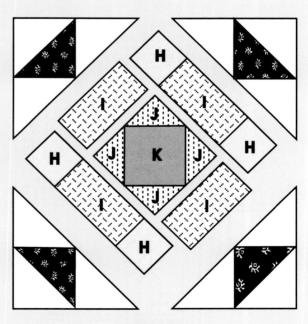

Join the long edge of one muslin D to each edge of the house. Then applique one fan to each outside corner of the muslin Ds to complete the house block (Diagram 3).

2. **Make center section.** Cut the following fabrics:
Four of Template F from muslin
Four 1" x 18" strips from tan print
Eight 1" x 13" strips from tan print

Join one 18" tan strip to each diagonal edge of the house block. Then center and join the long edges of each Template F to the tan strips. (Each tan strip is ⅜" wide.) Center and stitch the 13" tan strip to the short edges of each Template F, adjusting as needed to make the corner of the fan block (Diagram 4). The outside edges of the center section must measure 24½" x 24½".

3. **Make corner fan blocks.** Cut the following fabrics:
Four 6½" x 6½" pieces from muslin
24 of Template B from assorted prints
Four of Template C from navy

Assemble four fans (Diagram 2). Applique one fan in the corner of each muslin piece.

Diagram 4

4. **Make Block 1.** Cut the following fabrics:
Four of Template G from navy print
12 of Template G from muslin
Four of Template H from navy
Four of Template I from navy plaid
Four of Template J from rose print
One of Template K from tan floral

Join one navy-print G to three muslin Gs (Diagram 5). Repeat to make four corner sets. Assemble the center section (Diagram 6). Then join the corner sets to the center section to complete the block.

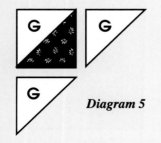

Diagram 5

Diagram 6

5. Make Block 2 (working clockwise). Cut the following fabrics:
One 6½" x 6½" piece from muslin
Four of Template L from red/black print
12 of Template M from tan print
Four ¾" x 3" bias strips from navy

Refer to Diagram 7 for placement of all pieces. Draw lines to divide the muslin piece in quarters. Draw a 4"-wide circle in the center of the muslin piece. Applique the navy bias strips over the circle in each quarter of the block. Applique the red/black-print Ls, centering each at the intersections of the quarter marks and circle. Applique the tan-print Ms to complete the block.

Diagram 7

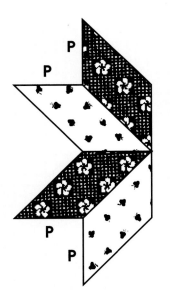

Diagram 8

6. Make Block 3. Cut the following fabrics:
Four of Template N from muslin
Four of Template O from muslin
Four of Template P from navy print
Four of Template P from tan print

Join one navy-print P and one tan-print P on the long edges. Repeat to make four P/P sets. Join two sets on the short edges to make half of the star (Diagram 8), then join the halves. Add muslin Ns and Os by hand (Diagram 9) to complete the block.

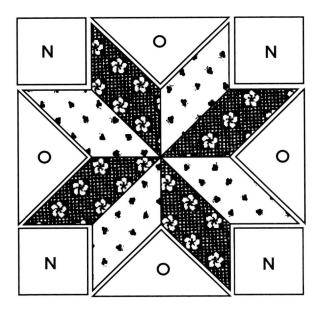

Diagram 9

7. **Make Block 4.** Cut the following fabrics:
Four of Template Q from muslin
Four of Template R from muslin
Four of Template Q from red/black print
Four of Template R from dusty-blue print
One of Template R from tan print

Join one muslin Q to one red/black-print Q on the long edges. Repeat to make four Q/Q sets. Join one muslin R to one dusty-blue R. Repeat to make four R/R sets. Join the two Q/Q sets to one R/R set (Diagram 10). Repeat to make two sets. Join the rows to complete the block, placing the tan-print R in the center (Diagram 11).

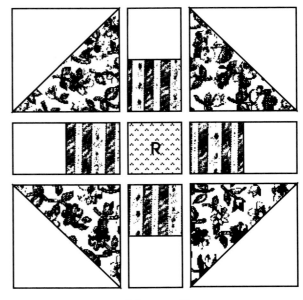

Diagram 11

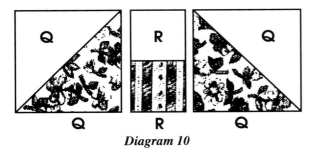

Diagram 10

8. **Make Block 5.** Cut the following fabrics:
Eight of Template S from muslin
Four of Template J from navy print
Four of Template T from navy print
Four of Template U from red pindot
One of Template V from tan floral

(This block should be pieced by hand.) Join one navy-print T to the diagonal edge of one red pindot U (Diagram 12). Repeat to make four sets. Stitch one U/T set to one edge of the tan floral V. Continue to add U/T sets (Diagram 13). Join one navy-print J to one diagonal edge of a muslin S (Diagram 14). Repeat to make four sets. Join a second muslin S to a J/S set to make a corner of the block. Repeat to make four sets. Join J/S/S sets to complete the block (Diagram 15).

Diagram 14

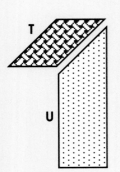

Diagram 12

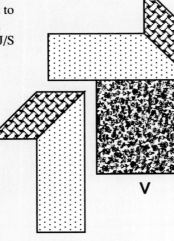

Diagram 13

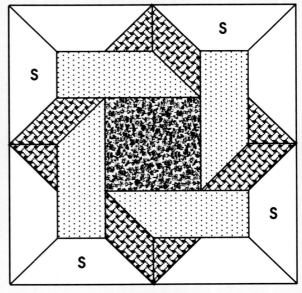

Diagram 15

9. **Make Block 6.** Cut the following fabrics:
One 6½" x 6½" piece from muslin
One BONNET from rose print
One DRESS from rose print
One ARM from rose print
One BONNET BRIM from navy plaid
One APRON from cream/rose print
Two HANDs from tan print
One FOOT from navy

Refer to Diagram 16 for placement of all pieces. Applique the navy foot to the muslin with the finished bottom edge centered ½" above the lower edge of the muslin. Applique the rose dress, then one tan hand before appliquing the cream/rose apron. Applique the navy plaid bonnet brim, then the rose bonnet. Applique the rose arm and the second tan hand to complete the block.

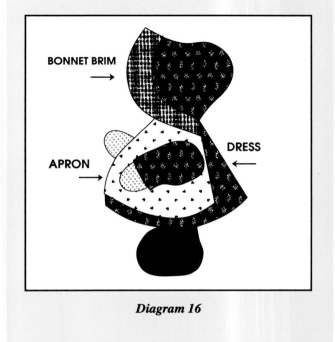

Diagram 16

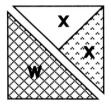

Diagram 17

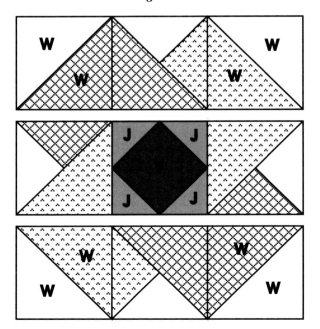

Diagram 18

10. **Make Block 7.** Cut the following fabrics:
Four of Template W from muslin
Four of Template X from muslin
Four of Template W from red pindot
Two of Template X from red pindot
Four of Template W from red/tan print
Two of Template X from red/tan print
Four of Template J from tan print
One of Template Y from navy print

Join one red pindot X to one muslin X on the short edges. Then join the X/X set to the long edge of one red/tan-print W (Diagram 17). Repeat to make two sets. Join one red/tan-print X to one muslin X on the short edges. Then join the X/X set to the long edge of one red pindot W (Diagram 17). Repeat to make two sets.

Join the long edges of one muslin W and one red/tan-print W. Repeat to make two sets. Join the long edges of one muslin W and one red pindot W. Repeat to make two sets.

Join one tan-print J to each edge of the navy-print Y to make the center section. Then join the sets to make three rows (Diagram 18). Join the rows to complete the block.

Diagram 19

11. **Make Block 8.** Cut the following fabrics:
   One 6½" x 6½" piece from muslin
   Four LEAFs from tan print
   Four of Template Z from tan print
   One of Template AA from red/black print

   Refer to Diagram 19 for placement of all pieces.
   Draw lines from corner to corner to divide the
   muslin piece in quarters. Applique the red/black-
   print AA to the center of the muslin piece. Then
   applique the four tan-print Zs between points of
   AA. Applique the tan-print leaves to the points of
   the AA to complete the block.

12. **Make Block 9.** Cut the following fabrics:
   One 6½" x 6½" piece from muslin
   Four ¾" x 2" bias strips from navy
   Four of Template BB from red pindot
   Four of Template CC from tan floral
   Eight of Template DD from tan floral

   Refer to Diagram 20 for placement of all pieces. Draw
   lines to divide the muslin piece in quarters. Draw a 3½"-
   wide circle in the center of the muslin piece. Applique the
   navy bias strips over the circle in each quarter of the block.
   Applique the red pindot BBs, centering each at the intersection of quarter marks and circle. Applique the tan floral
   CCs in the center of each BB. Applique the tan floral DDs
   in pairs outside the circle to complete the block.

Diagram 20

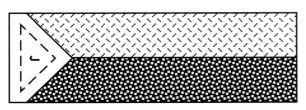

Diagram 21

13. **Make Block 10.** Cut the following fabrics:
   Four of Template G from navy plaid
   12 of Template G from muslin
   One of Template K from navy print
   Four of Template EE from dusty-blue print
   One 1" x 6" strip from tan print
   One 1" x 6" strip from red/black print

   Join one navy-plaid G and three muslin Gs (Diagram
   5, pg. 24). Repeat to make four corner sets. To make
   small triangles in center section, join the tan-print and
   red/black-print strips on the long edges. Place Template J over the strips (Diagram 21). Cut four triangles.

Join the long edge of each triangle pair to the edges of the navy-print K. Then assemble the center section (Diagram 22). Join the corner sets to edge of each dusty blue EE (Diagram 23) to complete the block.

Diagram 22

Diagram 23

14. Make Block 11. Cut the following fabrics:
One 6½" x 6½" piece from muslin
Eight of Template DD from navy
One of Template FF from navy print
One of Template GG from red/tan print
One of Template HH from rose print
Four of Template II from cream/rose print

Refer to Diagram 24 for placement of all pieces. Draw lines from corner to corner to divide the muslin piece in quarters. Applique the cream/rose-print IIs on the diagonal lines, placing stems ¾" from center of block. Center the rose-print HH in the block and applique. Then center and applique the red/tan GG and navy-print FF over the previous layer. Applique the navy DDs to complete the block.

Diagram 24

15. Make Block 12. Cut the following fabrics:
Four of Template K from muslin
Eight of Template J from muslin
Eight of Template J from red/black print
Eight of Template J from navy print
Four of Template H from rose print
Four of Template G from tan print
One 2⅛" x 2⅛" piece from navy print

Assemble one side set (Diagram 25). Repeat to make four side sets. Join one muslin K to each end of two side sets to make the top and bottom rows of the block (Diagram 26). Join the tan-print Gs to each edge of the navy-print square to make the center set, then join the remaining side sets to the opposite edges of the center set to make the center row (Diagram 26). Join the rows to complete the block.

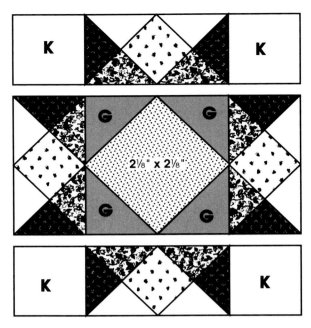

Diagram 26

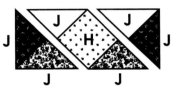

Diagram 25

Diagram 27

16. Make Block 13. Cut the following fabrics:
One 6½" x 6½" piece from muslin
Four of Template KK from red/tan print
Four of Template LL from navy print
Two ¾" x 2¼" bias strips from navy

Refer to Diagram 27 for placement of the pieces. Draw lines from corner to corner to divide the muslin piece in quarters. Center and applique the navy bias strips on the diagonal lines. Applique one red/tan-print KK to the end of each bias strip. Then applique one navy-print LL at the inside corners of the bias strips to complete the block.

17. Make Block 14. Cut the following fabrics:
Four of Template MM from muslin
Four of Template NN from muslin
Four of Template OO from muslin
Four of Template NN from red/black print
Four of Template UU from red/black print
Four of Template QQ from tan floral
One of Template RR from navy print

Assemble the center section (Diagram 28). Then assemble one side set (Diagram 29). Repeat to make four side sets. Join one muslin MM to each end of two side sets to make the top and bottom rows of the block (Diagram 30). Join the remaining side sets to opposite edges of the center section to make the center row. Join the rows to complete the block.

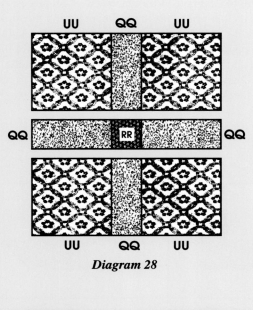

Diagram 28

Diagram 29

Diagram 30

Diagram 31

18. Make Block 15. Cut the following fabrics:
One 6½" x 6½" piece from muslin
One HAT from dusty-blue print
One POCKET from dusty-blue print
One SHIRT from tan print
One OVERALLS from red plaid
Two FEET from navy

Refer to Diagram 31 for placement of all pieces. Applique the tan-print shirt to muslin, centering the top edge of the shirt 2" below the top edge of the block. Using the red-plaid overalls as a guide, find placement for the navy feet and applique. Applique the red-plaid overalls, then the dusty-blue-print hat. Applique the pocket to complete the block.

19. Make Block 16. Cut the following fabrics:
Eight 1" x 1¾" pieces from muslin
Four of Template NN from muslin
Four of Template R from muslin
Eight of Template SS from navy print
Eight of Template SS from red pindot
Four of Template VV from tan print
One of Template TT from tan print

Join one navy-print SS and red pindot SS on one long edge. Repeat to make eight sets. Then join the navy-print pieces on the diagonal edge (Diagram 32).

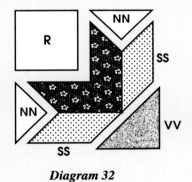

Diagram 32

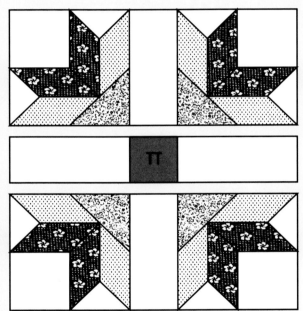

Diagram 33

Assemble one corner set (Diagram 32). Repeat to make four corner sets. Join the corner sets to the 1" x 1¾" muslin pieces to make the top and bottom rows of the block (Diagram 33). Join two muslin pieces to the tan-print TT to make the center row (Diagram 33). Join the rows to complete the block.

20. Make quilt top. Join the blocks in numerical sequence to the center house block, then join the corner blocks; see Diagram 34.

21. Add border. Cut the following fabrics:
Four 2¾" x 42" strips from tan/rose print
4¾ yards of 1¼"-wide bias strips from navy

Center and stitch one navy strip to one side of the quilt, stopping ¼" from the edge of the top. Repeat for all four sides. Miter the corners. Make 4¾ yards of corded piping from the navy bias strips. Stitch the corded piping to the outside edge of the border, rounding the corners slightly.

22. **Mark quilting lines.** Mark all quilting lines (Diagram 34). (The Pineapple Quilting Pattern and the Fan Quilting Pattern are on pages 40-41.) Mark echo quilting lines ¼" apart outside each pineapple motif to fill the triangle. Mark a 1"-wide diamond grid on the muslin background of blocks 2, 6, 8, 9, 11, 13 and 15, the corner fan blocks and the house block.

23. **Complete the quilt.** Cut the following fabrics:
One 43" x 43" piece from cream/rose print for backing
One 43" x 43" piece from polyester fleece

Layer the quilt backing (wrong side up), fleece and quilt top. Baste. Quilt on all marked lines. Using cream thread, quilt in-the-ditch around all pieces in blocks 2, 6, 8, 9, 11, 13 and 15. Trim the backing and fleece to match the edges of the cording. Fold the cording and backing ¼" to the inside. Slipstitch the entire edge of the quilt. ❖

•••••••••••••••••••••• *Navy thread*
- - - - - - - - - - - - *Cream thread*

Diagram 34

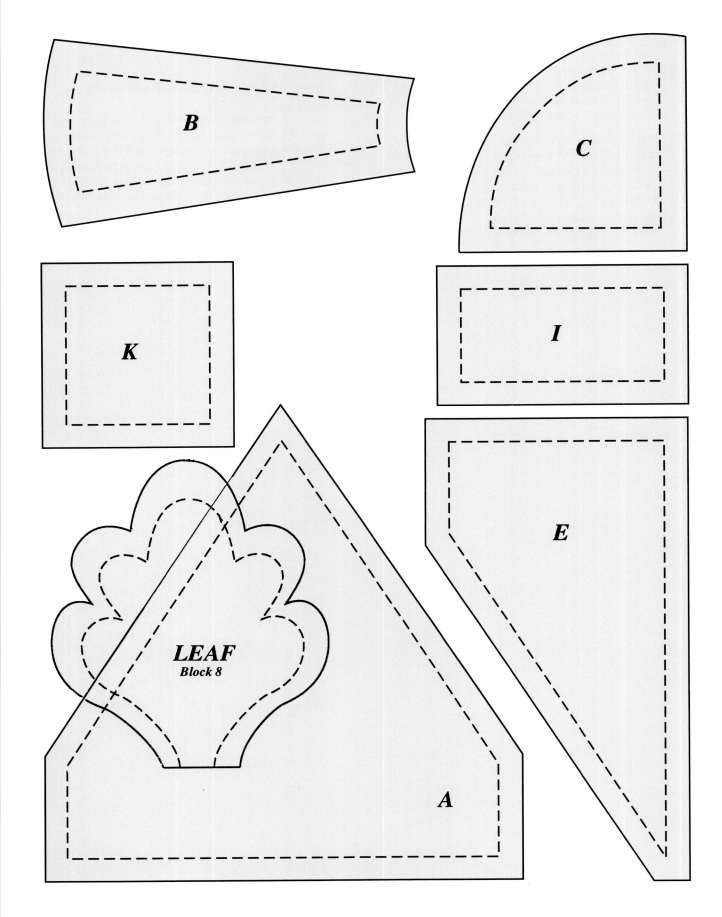

B

C

K

I

LEAF
Block 8

E

A

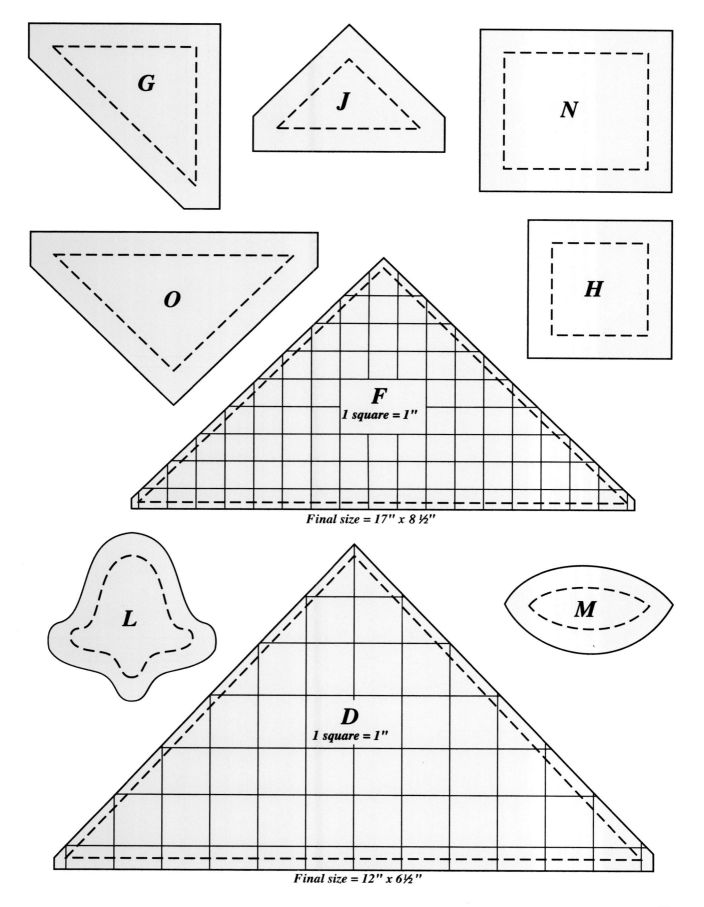

G

J

N

O

H

F
1 square = 1"
Final size = 17" x 8 ½"

L

M

D
1 square = 1"
Final size = 12" x 6½"

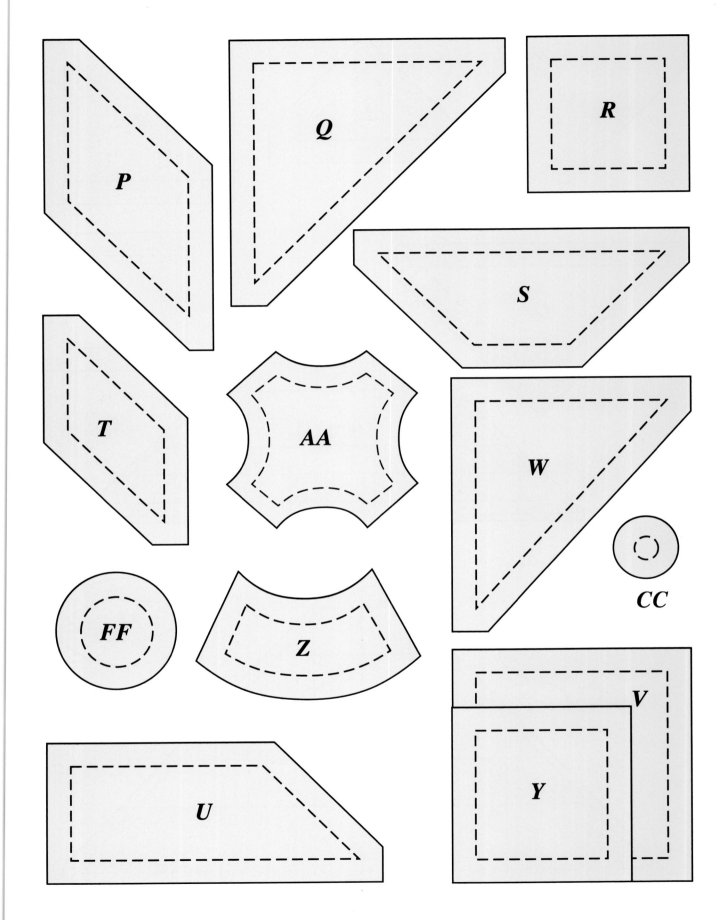

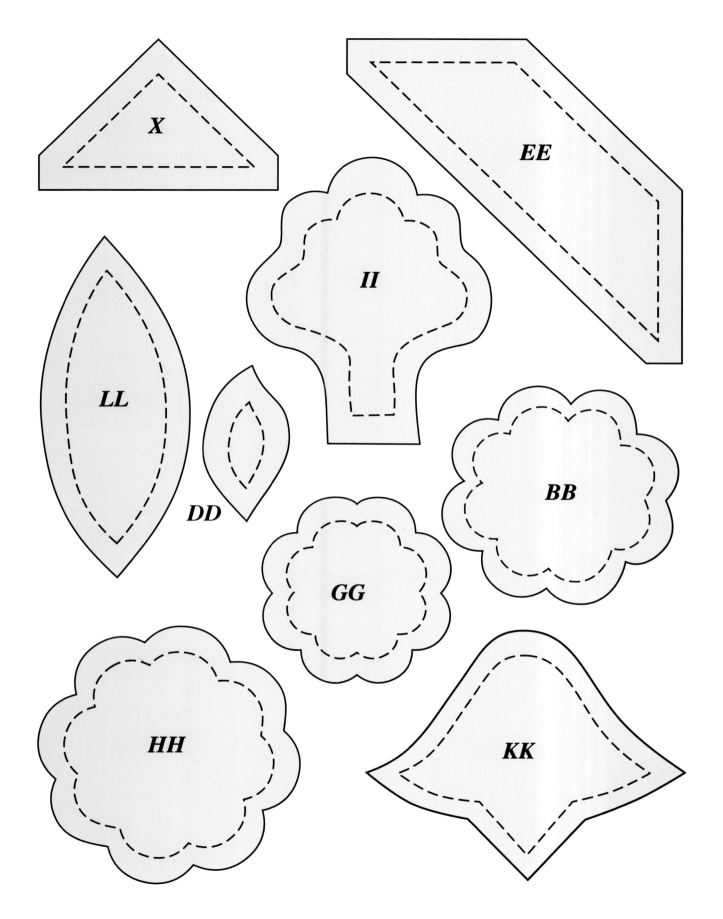

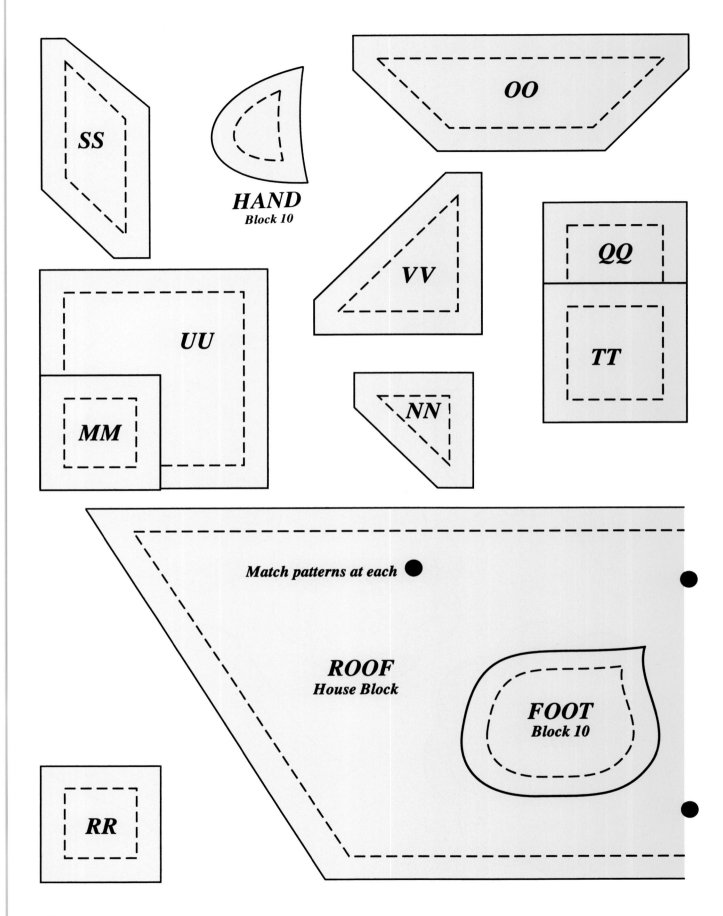

SS

HAND
Block 10

OO

VV

QQ

TT

UU

MM

NN

RR

ROOF
House Block

Match patterns at each ●

FOOT
Block 10

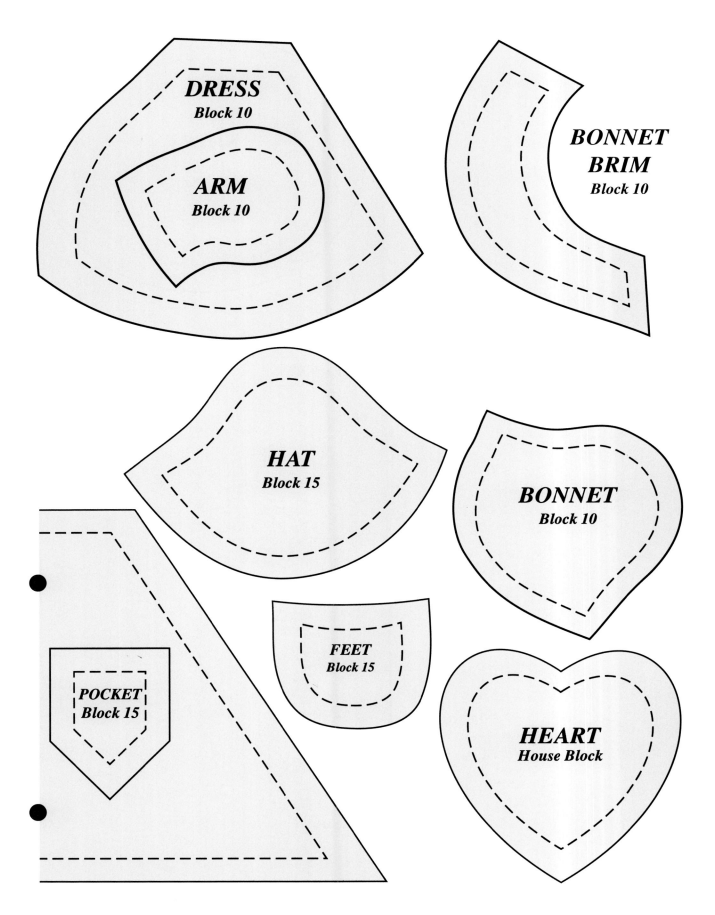

DRESS
Block 10

ARM
Block 10

BONNET BRIM
Block 10

HAT
Block 15

BONNET
Block 10

POCKET
Block 15

FEET
Block 15

HEART
House Block

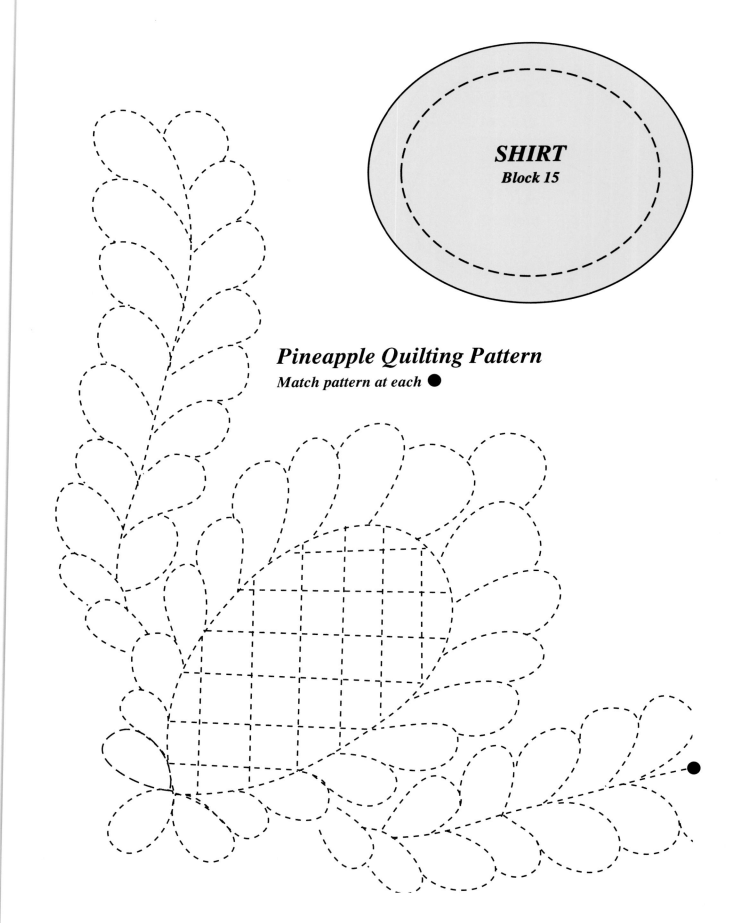

SHIRT
Block 15

Pineapple Quilting Pattern
Match pattern at each ●

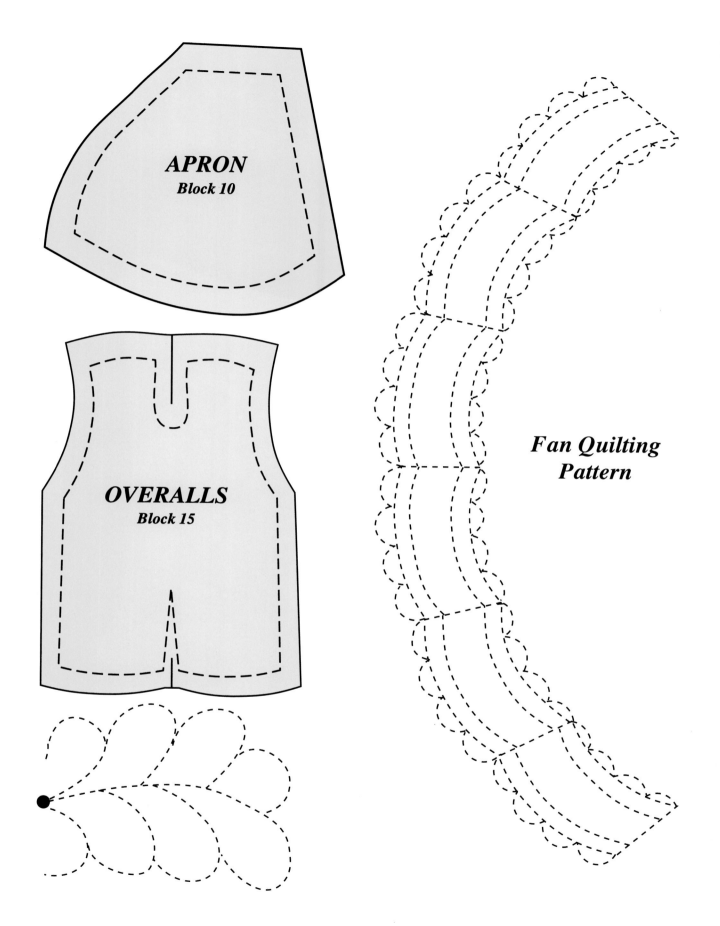

APRON
Block 10

OVERALLS
Block 15

Fan Quilting Pattern

Check Mates

Pillow #1 (two yellow hearts):

Finished size: 13½" x 13½"

Materials:

½ yard of muslin:
    One 2" x 26" strip
    One 14" x 14" inner piece

½ yard of blue-print fabric:
    One 2" x 26" strip
    One 14" x 14" backing piece

¼ yard of gray fabric:
    Eight 1" x 15" border strips

¼ yard of gray-print fabric:
    Four 2½" x 15" border strips

Scrap of bright-yellow fabric:
    Two HEARTs, adding ¼" seam allowance

⅜ yard of yellow pindot fabric:
    56" of 1½"-wide bias for corded piping

One 14" x 14" pillow form
One 14" x 14" piece of polyester fleece
Gray thread for construction
1⅝ yards of medium cording
Embroidery floss to match blue-print fabric

Pillow # 2 (four yellow hearts):

Finished size: 11½" x 11½"

Materials for Pillow #2 (four yellow hearts):

½ yard of muslin:
    One 2" x 26" strip
    One 12" x 12" inner piece
    Four 1" x 13" border strips
    56" of 1½"-wide bias for corded piping

⅜ yard of blue-print fabric:
    One 2" x 26" strip
    Four 2" x 13" border strips
    One 12" x 12" backing piece

Scrap of yellow pindot fabric:
    Four HEARTs, adding ¼" seam allowance

One 12" x 12" pillow form
One 12" x 12" piece of polyester fleece
Gray thread for construction
1⅝ yards of medium cording
Embroidery floss to match blue-print fabric

Pillow #3 (three yellow hearts):

Finished size: 10" x 10"

Materials:

½ yard of muslin:
    One 2" x 26" strip
    One 10½" x 10½" inner piece

½ yard of blue-print fabric:
    One 2" x 26" strip

⅛ yard of gray-print fabric:
    Four 1¼" x 13" border strips

⅛ yard of gray fabric:
    Four 1" x 13" border strips

¼ yard of white-with-blue print:
    Four 1¾" x 13" border strips
    One 10½" x 10½" backing piece

Scrap of bright-yellow fabric:
    Three HEARTs, adding ¼" seam allowance
    56" of 1½"-wide bias for corded piping

One 11" x 11" pillow form
One 10½" x 10½" piece of polyester fleece
Gray thread for construction
1⅝ yards of medium cording
Embroidery floss to match blue-print fabric

Dreamy hearts and stars fill the checkerboard tops of each of these adorable pillows. Although you can't see it in the photo, some of the borders and backs of the pillows are made from the wrong side of the fabric to achieve a washed-out look. Check it out for yourself!

Directions (for one pillow):

1. **Make checkerboard center.** Join the 2" x 26" blue-print and muslin strips on the long edges. Cut the strips into 2"-wide segments. Join the segments to make five rows of five squares each (Diagram 1). Join the rows to make the checkerboard center.

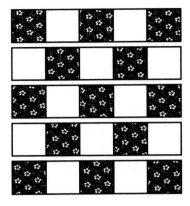

Diagram 1

2. **Applique hearts.** Applique one bright-yellow HEART to the center of each designated muslin square (two for Pillow #1, three for Pillow #2 and four for Pillow #3); see schematics.

3. **Embroider design.** To mark the placement for each heart design, trace one HEART in the center of each remaining muslin square. With one strand of floss, chain stitch the outline of each traced heart. Embroider smyrna cross stars at random in each heart square.

4. **Add border.** *Pillow #1*: Join one long edge each of two gray border strips to both long edges of one gray-print border strip. Repeat to make four gray/gray-print/gray border sets. Join the border sets to the sides of the pillow top, matching the centers. Miter the corners.

   Pillow #2: Join the long edges of one blue-print border strip (wrong side up) and one muslin border strip. Repeat to make four border sets. Join the muslin side of the border sets to the sides of the pillow top, matching the centers. Miter the corners.

   Pillow #3: Join the long edges of one white-with-blue border strip, one gray-print border strip and one gray border strip. Repeat to make four border sets. Join the gray side of the border sets to the sides of the pillow top, matching the centers. Miter the corners.

5. **Complete pillow top.** Layer the muslin inner piece, fleece and pillow top (right side up). Baste. Machine quilt in-the-ditch on each seam.

6. **Complete pillow.** Make 56" of corded piping from yellow pindot bias for pillows #1 and #2, and muslin bias for pillow #3. Stitch corded piping to the raw edges of the pillow top. Stitch the pillow top to the pillow back (wrong side up for pillows #1 and #3), sewing on the stitching line of piping and leaving a large opening in one edge. Insert the pillow form. Slipstitch the opening closed. ❖

Schematic for Pillow #1

Schematic for Pillow #2

Schematic for Pillow #3

Sew and Stow Basket

Do you go crazy when you sit down to sew and can't find your favorite scissors, needles, pins, scraps, threads, and buttons? Well, store them in our crazy-quilted sewing basket, and you'll never have to hunt for them again!

Finished size: 21" x 23"

Materials:

⅝ yard of blue-print fabric:
   One TOP for backing piece (see Step 1)

1 yard of matching blue-print fabric (double-faced quilted):
   One LINER (see Step 1)
   One BOTTOM, adding 2" to outside edges (see Step 1)

Scraps of assorted pink-, blue-, and green-print fabrics:
   Pieces in different shapes for crazy-quilt top

Scrap of burgundy fabric:
   One BEAR
   Two SMALL HEARTs

Scrap of dark-blue fabric:
   One BOW

Scrap of green fabric:
   One STEM
   Two LEAFs

Scrap of pink fabric:
   One TULIP
   One LARGE HEART

Scrap of organdy fabric:
   One 8" x 8" piece

Scrap of maroon fabric:
   One BEAR HEART

Scrap of muslin:
   One 8" x 8" piece
   Two INNER EARs
   Two SMALL PAWs
   Two LARGE PAWs
   One MOUTH

Scrap of batting:
   One BOTTOM (see Step 1)

Scrap of corrugated cardboard:
   One BOTTOM (see Step 1)

⅝ yard of flannel
1¾ yards of ¾"-wide eyelet beading
4 yards of ⅜"-wide pink satin ribbon
3¾ yards of 1½"-wide gathered
   cream lace
Embroidery flosses in different colors
Fusing material
Two or three purchased appliques
Small amounts of lace trim
Thread

Directions:

1. **Make patterns.** To make the LINER pattern, measure around the top edge of the basket. Also measure the depth of the basket. Make the pattern with these measurements, adding 1" to the top edge measurement and 4" to the depth measurement.

   To make the BOTTOM pattern, measure the inside bottom of the basket. Make the pattern with these measurements.

   To make the TOP pattern, place a large piece of paper on a table top, aligning the edges. Then place the basket upside down over the edge of the table, with the handles butting against the table. Trace around the basket edge. Turn the paper and repeat for the second half of the basket, allowing space for the handles. Make the pattern, adding 2½" outside the traced line.

2. **Line basket.** Stitch the short ends of the blue-print LINER with right sides together. Place the liner inside the basket, folding the outer edge of the liner 2" over the basket edge; check the fit. (If the liner seems too full on the inside, fold the excess into a large dart in each corner; stitch on the wrong side.) Mark placement for the basket handles.

Cut a U-shaped opening on each side for the handles. Fold under ¼" and stitch. Stitch lace to the right side of all edges except the openings for the handles. Stitch the eyelet beading over the edge of lace. Thread the ribbon through the beading, beginning and ending at each handle opening and leaving 5" ribbon tails. Place the liner in the basket, folding the outer edge of the liner over the basket edge. Tie the ribbon tails into bows around the handles.

Zigzag around the edges of the blue-print BOTTOM. Layer the wrong side of the blue-print BOTTOM and the batting BOTTOM. Sew running stitches around the edge. Place the cardboard BOTTOM against the batting. Draw up the running stitches tightly, pulling the fabric/batting over the cardboard; secure. Place in the bottom of the basket.

3. **Make bear patch.** Fuse the BEAR HEART, INNER EARs, MOUTH and all PAWs to the burgundy BEAR (see pattern for placement). Fuse the BEAR to the muslin piece. Place the organdy piece over the bear and baste to muslin. Using black floss, French knot the eyes and nose, then embroider the mouth (Diagram 1). Using a contrasting floss, embroider the bow (Diagram 1). Using a different contrasting floss, quilt all remaining marked lines through all layers (Diagram 1).

Diagram 1

4. **Make basket top.** Trace the TOP pattern onto the flannel. Crazy quilt the bear patch onto the flannel. Then crazy quilt the assorted pink-, blue-, and green-print fabric pieces onto the flannel.

Applique the BOW, LARGE HEART, SMALL HEARTs, TULIP, STEM, and two LEAFs (one on each side of the stem) where desired. Attach the purchased appliques where desired. Using dark-blue floss, embroider lines on the bow (Diagram 2). Embellish all of the basket-top seams with various embroidery stitches worked with contrasting colors of floss (see photo).

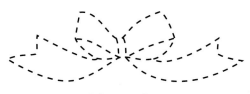

Diagram 2

Cut one TOP from the crazy-quilted piece. Stitch lace to the right side edges with fullness toward the inside. Layer the crazy-quilted TOP and blue-print TOP backing piece with right sides together. Cut a U-shaped opening for each handle. Stitch around all outside edges of the top, leaving an opening. Clip the corners and seam allowances around handle openings. Turn. Slipstitch opening closed.

Place the design piece over the top of the basket (see photo) and mark placement for the ribbon ties at handles. Tack ribbons securely to the design piece. Tie the ribbons around the handles. ❖

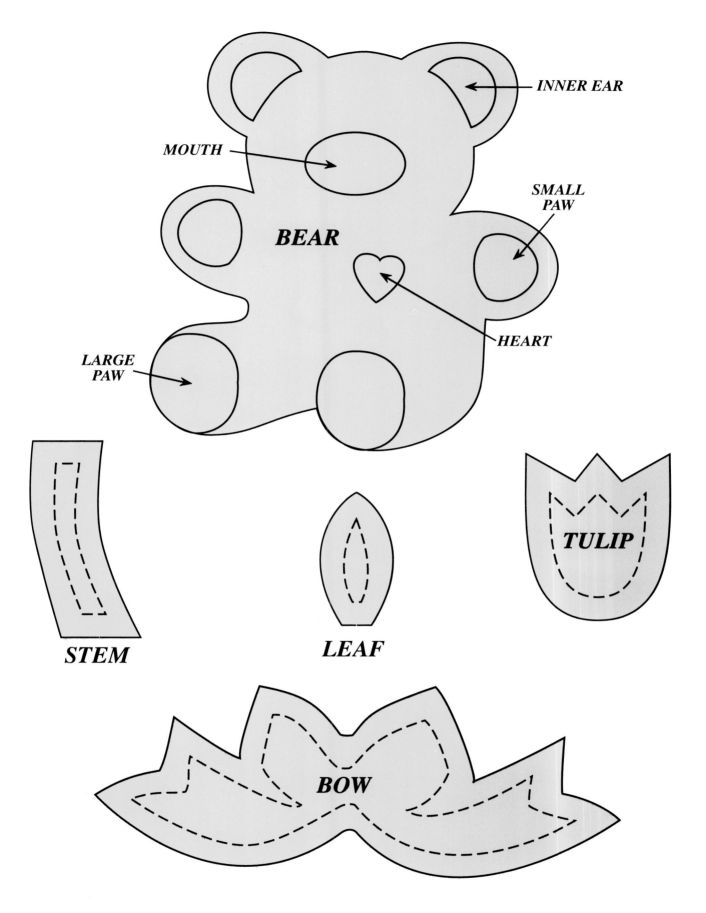

INNER EAR

MOUTH

SMALL PAW

BEAR

HEART

LARGE PAW

STEM

LEAF

TULIP

BOW

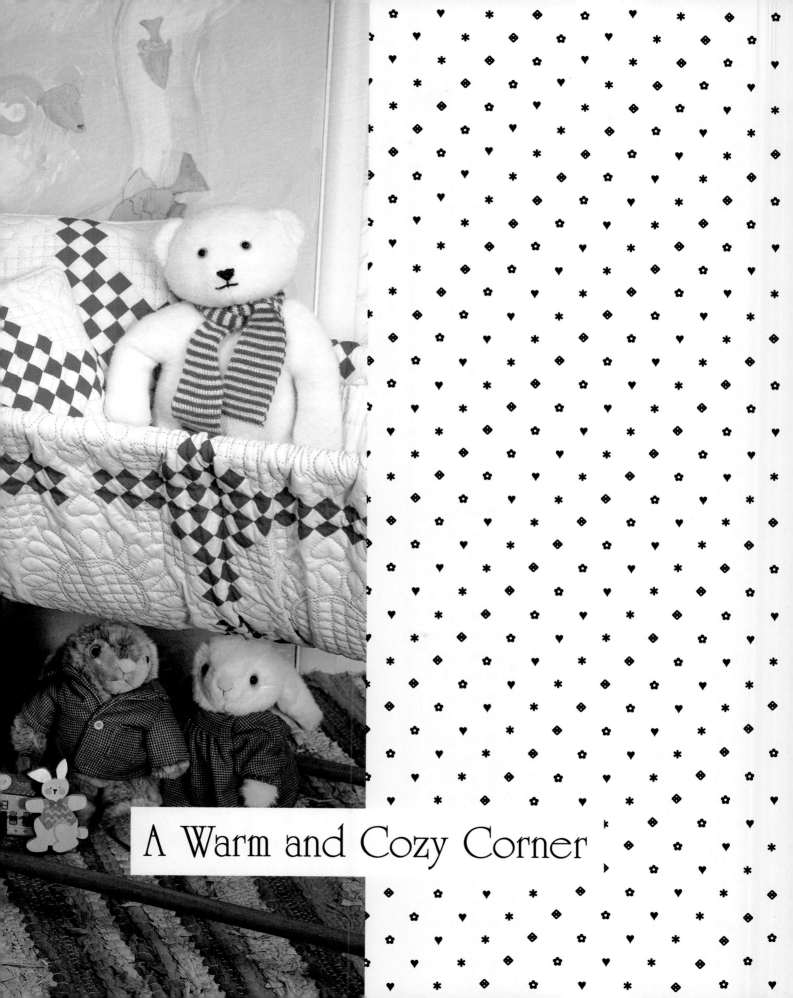

A Warm and Cozy Corner

Country Cradle

Lay baby down to sleep in the comfort of this cozy homespun cradle set. We even show you how to construct the cradle itself!

Finished size: 36" x 60"

Materials:

¾ yard of red fabric:
  21 1¼" x 44" strips

5½ yards of muslin:
  21 1¼" x 44" strips
  60 2" x 4¼" pieces
  20 9" x 9" pieces
  One 38" x 62" backing piece
  Two 5" x 62" strips
  Two 5" x 38" strips
  Two 16½" x 36" pieces for mattress

2¾ yard of polyester fleece:
  One 36" x 60" piece
  One 32½" x 36" piece

Polyester stuffing

Cream thread for construction
Red thread for quilting
12' of 1" x 2½" birch
Eight 2" brass screws
Eight brass washers (to use with screws)
Four 1" x 36" dowels
Two ¼" x 2½" bolts
Two ¼" nuts
Two ¼" washers
Two ⅜" x 26" welding rods
Drill
1/16" Drill bit
¼" Drill bit
Sandpaper
Stain
Varnish
Paint brush
Gold spray paint

Directions:

1. **Construct checkerboards blocks.** Join the long edges of the 1¼"-wide muslin and red strips. Cut these into 1¼"-wide segments. Join the segments to make seven rows of seven squares each (Diagram 1). Join the rows to make one middle set. Repeat to make 15 middle sets.

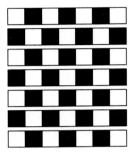

Diagram 1

Make 60 corner sections (Diagram 2). Join one corner section to each end of a 2" x 4¼" muslin piece to make one corner set (Diagram 3). Repeat to make 30 corner sets.

Diagram 2   *Diagram 3*

Then join one segment to each end of a 2" x 4¼" muslin piece to make one side set (Diagram 4). Repeat to make 30 side sets. Join two side sets to one middle set. Then join two corner sets to the middle sets to make one checkerboard block (Diagram 5). Repeat to make 15 checkerboard blocks.

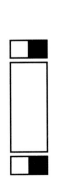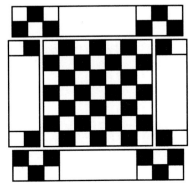

Diagram 4   *Diagram 5*

2. Make quilt top. Join the checkerboard blocks to the 9" x 9" muslin pieces to make seven rows (Diagram 6).

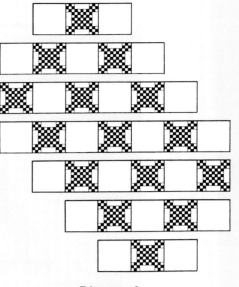

Diagram 6

Join all of the rows to make the quilt top. Trim the quilt top through the center of each muslin block on the outside edges (Diagram 7).

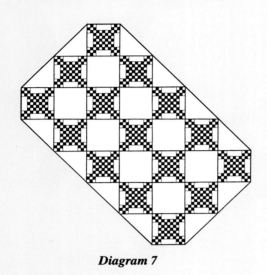

Diagram 7

3. Complete cradle quilt. Trace the Flower Quilting Pattern and the Heart Quilting Pattern in the center of each muslin block (Diagram 8). Also mark a diamond grid in each 2" x 4¼" muslin piece (Diagram 9). Mark all lines that intersect from corner-to-corner through two rows of the red pieces in each checkerboard.

Layer the quilt back (wrong side up), fleece and quilt top. Baste. Quilt all marked lines with red thread.

4. Make mattress. Fold the 32½" x 36" fleece piece to measure 16¼"-wide. Stitch all of the edges, leaving a small opening. Turn. Stuff moderately. Stitch the opening closed. Stitch the muslin mattress pieces with right sides together, leaving an opening. Turn. Insert the fleece. Slipstitch the opening closed.

Diagram 8

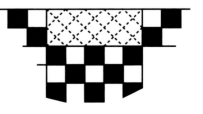

Diagram 9

5. **Make cradle.** (Refer to Diagram 10 for construction.) To make the legs, cut the 12' birch piece into four 34" pieces for the cradle stand, rounding the ends. Sand all of the edges. Drill a ¹⁄₁₆" hole in each leg 1" from one end and 3½" from the other end, centering both horizontally. Drill a ¼" hole in the center of each leg. Stain and varnish as desired.

To make the dowels, drill a ¹⁄₁₆" hole in the center of both ends of each dowel. Sand all surfaces. Stain and varnish as desired.

To make the rods, bend a 1" hook on both ends of each welding rod. Paint the rods gold.

Using brass washers with screws, screw one leg to two dowels through the ¹⁄₁₆" holes to make the cradle ends. Repeat with one leg and two dowels. Attach the remaining legs to the opposite end of the dowels. Match ¼" holes in the legs and fasten two legs together using the nuts and bolts and washers.

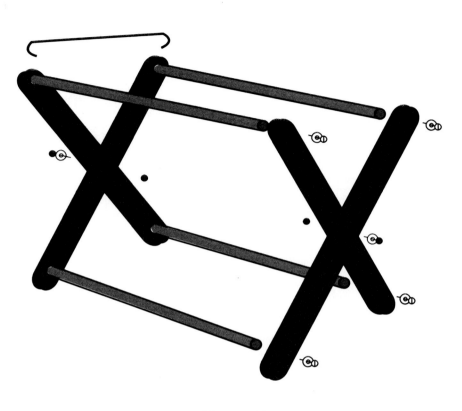

Diagram 10

6. **Attach quilt.** Stitch the purchased bias tape to the edge of the checkerboard block in each corner of the quilt. Fold the corner to the back; slipstitch. To make the casings, fold all muslin strips to measure 2½"-wide; press. Match raw edges to right side of one long edge; stitch. Fold these edges 2" to the quilt back and slipstitch securely. Repeat for remaining edges.

Feed the quilt onto the dowels and brass rods through the casing. Hook rods over the dowels at each end of the cradle (notch dowels if needed). Place the mattress in the bottom of the quilt.

Cradle Coverlet

Finished size: 31½" x 37½"

Materials:

2 yards of muslin:
    One 32" x 38" piece
    One 34" x 40" piece

½ yard of red fabric:
    3¼ yards of 1¼"-wide bias for corded piping

1 yard of polyester fleece
    One 34" x 40"

Cream thread for construction
Red thread for quilting
3¼ yards of small cording
Template for 4"- to 5"-wide x 30" feather border pattern

Directions:

1. **Mark quilt top.** Mark vertical and horizontal centers of one muslin quilt piece. Then mark off sections (Diagram 11). Mark quilting lines, using the quilting template in five diamond sections created by lines. Mark 1" grid in triangles on edge of marked sections, leaving 4" on each side and 7" on each end. Use border templates for each end.

2. **Complete quilt.** Layer the coverlet back (wrong side up), fleece and coverlet top. Baste. Quilt all marked lines with red thread (see Coverlet Schematic).

Make a pattern to round the corners slightly. Cut corners. Make 3¼ yards of red corded piping. Stitch to quilt top and fleece only. Trim fleece from seam allowance. Fold backing under ¼" and slipstitch to piping on all edges.

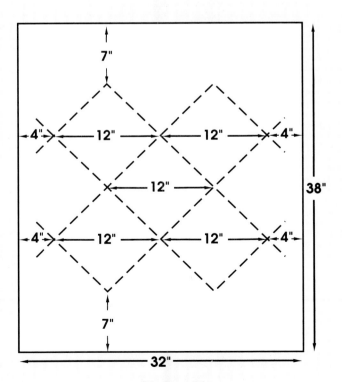

Diagram 11

Coverlet Schematic

Cradle Pillow

Finished size: 12" x 12"

Materials:

1¼ yards of muslin:
    Two 12" x 12" pieces
    Two 1¼" x 44" strips
    Four of Template A
    1½ yards of 2"-wide bias for
    corded piping.

⅛ yard of red fabric:
    Two 1¼" x 44" strips

⅜ yard of polyester fleece:
    One 12" x 12" piece

Cream thread for construction
Red quilting thread
1½ yards of medium cording
12" x 12" pillow form

Directions:

1. Construct pillow top. Complete Step 1 of the cradle quilt to make one checkerboard block. Add muslin As to each edge (Diagram 12).

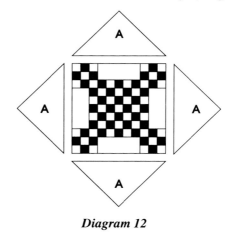

Diagram 12

2. Finish pillow. Mark quilting lines on muslin As using the Flower Quilting Pattern (see pillow schematic). Mark diamond pattern in 2" x 4¼" pieces and intersection, corner-to-corner lines (see Step 3 of cradle). Layer muslin, fleece and pillow top. Quilt all lines with red thread.

Make 52" of corded piping from muslin. Stitch the pillow top, using the stitching line of the piping and leaving an opening. Insert pillow form. Slipstitch the opening closed. ❖

Pillow Schematic

Flower Quilting Pattern

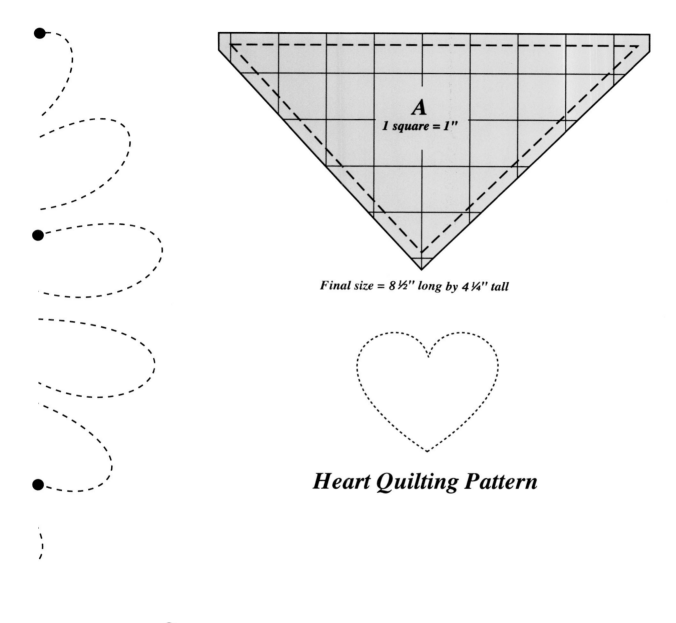

A
1 square = 1"

Final size = 8 ½" long by 4 ¼" tall

Heart Quilting Pattern

Match pattern at each ●

Star Light, Star Bright

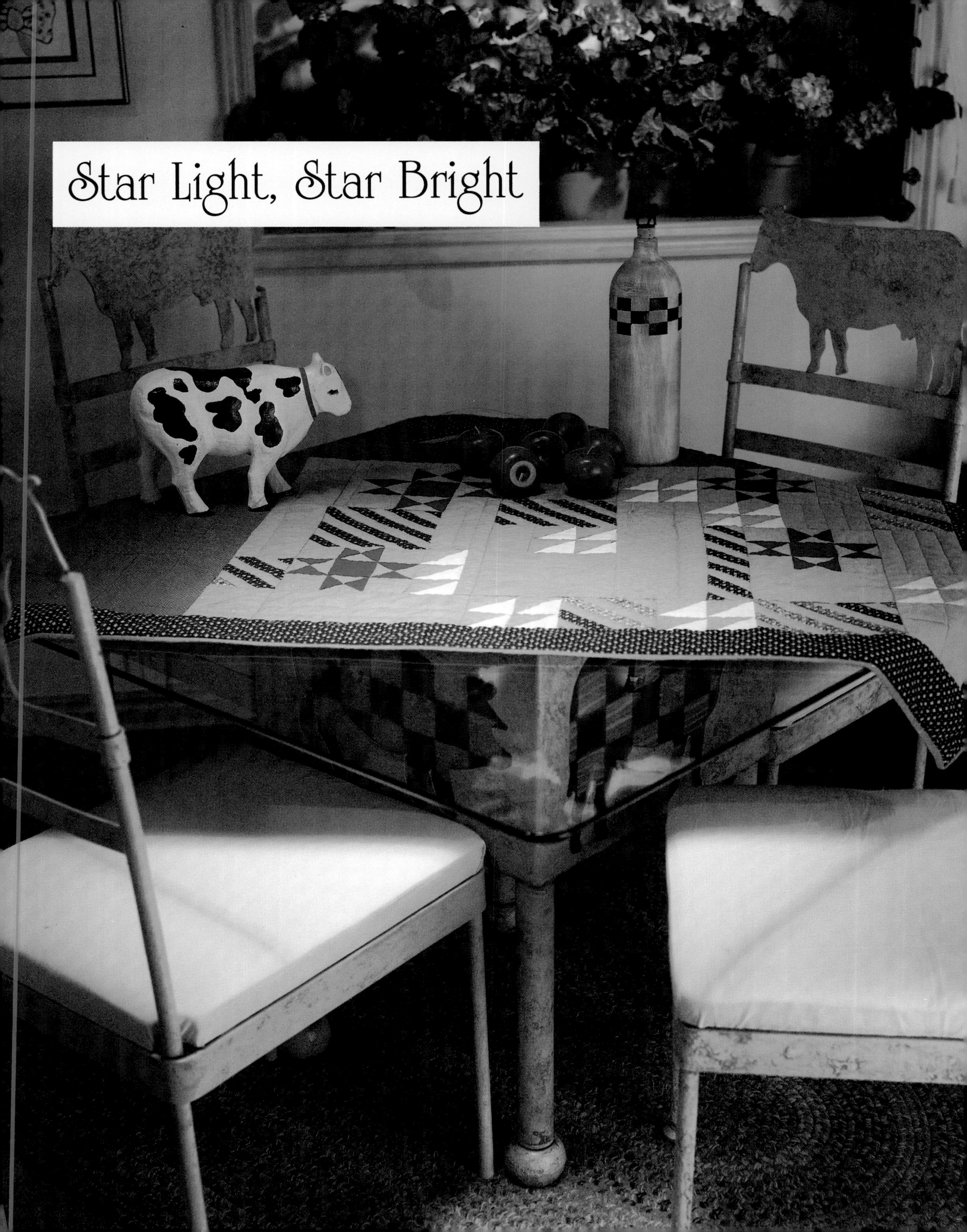

Directions:

1. **Make star blocks.** Note that the upper left star block is larger than the other three star blocks (see Diagram 12). The construction process is the same for all four.

Join one blue B to one aqua B on the short edges. Repeat to make eight sets. Then join the B/B sets on the long edges (Diagram 1). Join four B/B/B/B sets with four aqua As and one blue A to make three rows. Join the rows to make one large star block (Diagram 2).

Diagram 1

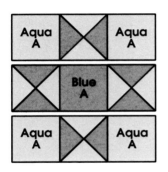

Diagram 2

Repeat the process above using the same colors, substituting Template C for Template A and Template D for Template B, to make three small star blocks.

2. **Make white triangle blocks.** Join one white E and one aqua E on the long edges. Repeat to make 27 E/E sets. Join four of the sets to make two rows, then join the rows to make one white triangle block (Diagram 3). Repeat to make six white triangle blocks. Join the three remaining sets in a strip (Diagram 4).

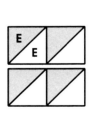

Diagram 3

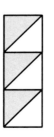

Diagram 4

You'll be seeing stars— and loving it—as you piece this unconventional blend of traditional quilt patterns in a kaleidescope of celestial colors.

Finished size: 38½" x 52½"

Materials:

¼ yard of blue fabric:
    One of Template A
    Eight of Template B
    Three of Template C
    24 of Template D

⅛ yard of white fabric:
    27 of Template E

3 yards of black-print fabric:
    13 1¼" x 22" strips
    Two 3¾" x 40" border strips
    Two 3¾" x 53" border strips
    One 40" x 54" backing piece

¾ yards of aqua fabric:
    15 1¼" x 22" strips
    Four of Template A
    Eight of Template B
    Twelve of Template C
    24 of Template D
    27 of Template E
    Pieces 1 through 17 (see Step 3)

⅝ yard of turquoise-print fabric:
    Six of Template F
    One 5" x 3½" piece
    One 1½" x 3½" piece
    One 9½" x 3½" piece
    One 33" x 4½" strip
    One 13½" x 31½" piece

1½ yards of batting:
    One 40" x 54" piece

Thread for construction
Aqua thread for quilting
5¼ yards of 1"-wide purchased gray bias
    tape for binding

3. **Make pieces for design section.** From aqua fabric, cut and label the following pieces:

#1	=	2½" x 16½"	#10 =	6½" x 6½"
#2	=	2½" x 4½"	#11 =	4½" x 8½"
#3	=	9" x 1½"	#12 =	4½" x 14½"
#4	=	1½" x 8"	#13 =	2½" x 6½"
#5	=	3" x 6"	#14 =	4½" x 4½"
#6	=	1" x 6½"	#15 =	6½" x 4½"
#7	=	9" x 4½"	#16 =	4½" x 6½"
#8	=	6½" x 6½"	#17 =	4½" x 4½"
#9	=	2½" x 4½"		

To make the diagonal stripe sets, join six 1¼"-wide black-print strips and seven 1¼"-wide aqua strips on the long edges, alternating the strips. Cutting on a 45° angle, cut and label the following pieces (save all of the scraps):

#18	= 6" x 6½"	#20	= 2½" x 10½"
#19	= 6½" x 4½"		

Next, join the wrong side of six 1¼"-wide black-print strips, the right side of one 1¼"-wide black-print strip, and the right side of eight 1¼"-wide aqua strips on the

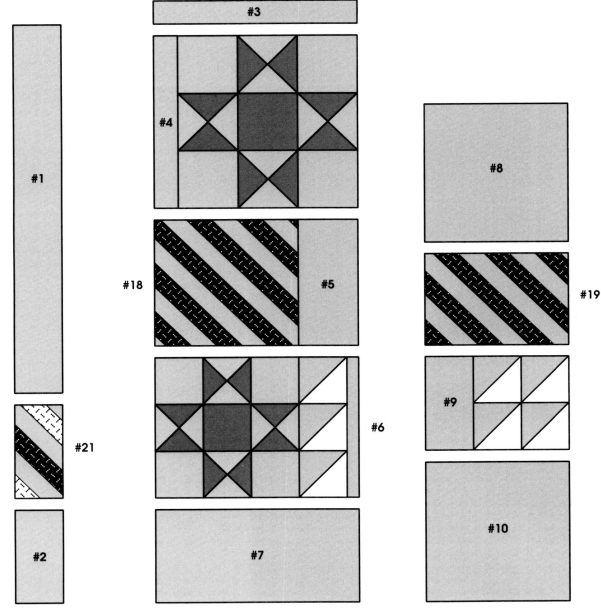

Diagram 5 - Section 1 *Diagram 6 - Section 2* *Diagram 7 - Section 3*

long edges, alternating the strips. Cutting on a 45°
angle, cut and label the following pieces (save all of
the scraps):

#21	=	2½" x 4½"	#23	=	4½" x 4½"
#22	=	4½" x 10½"	#24	=	6½" x 4½"

4. **Make design section.** Assemble Sections 1 through 7
as follows:

Section 1: (Diagram 5).

Section 2: Join #4 to the left edge of the large star
block. Join #5 to the right edge of #18. Join #6 to the
right edge of the white triangle strip; join this set to one
small star block. Complete the section (Diagram 6).

Section 3: Join #9 to the left edge of one white triangle
block. Complete the section (Diagram 7).

Section 4: (Diagram 8).

Section 5: Join #13 to the right edge of one small star
block. Join #14 to the right edge of one white triangle
block. Join #15 to the bottom edge of one small star
block; join this set to the right edge of #20. Complete
Section 5 (Diagram 9).

Section 6: (Diagram 10).

Section 7: (Diagram 11).

Join Sections 1 through 7 to complete the design
section (Diagram 12).

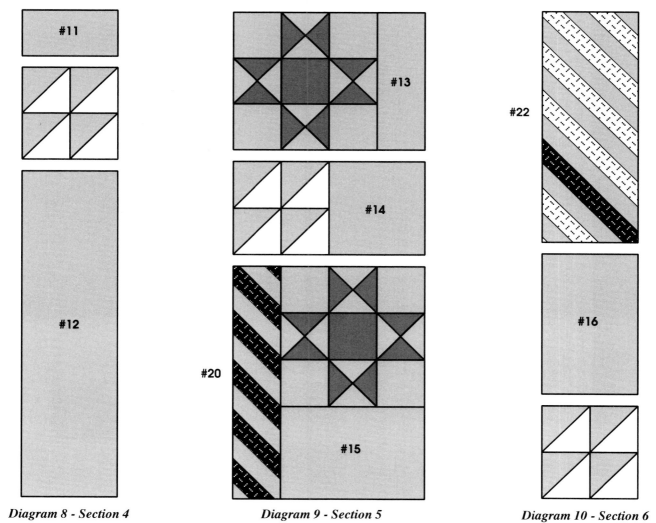

Diagram 8 - Section 4   *Diagram 9 - Section 5*   *Diagram 10 - Section 6*

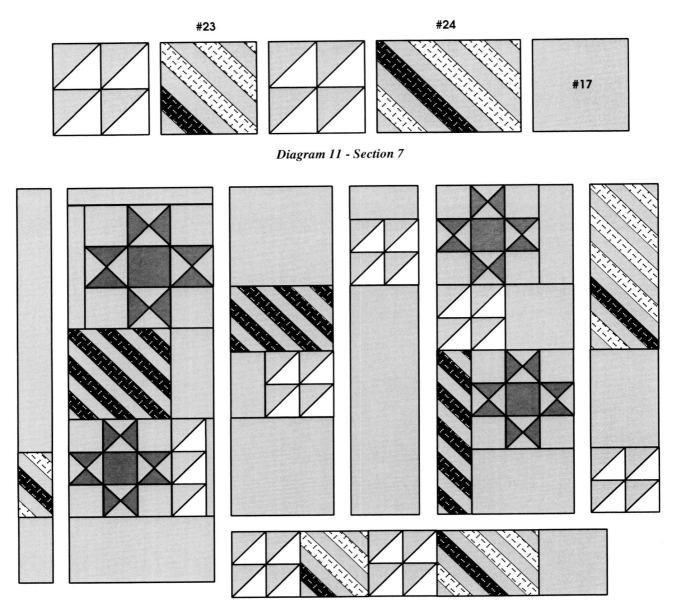

Diagram 11 - Section 7

Diagram 12

5. **Complete quilt top.** From the scraps of diagonal stripe blocks, cut six of Template F, noting the placement of the seams on the template, but allowing the right and wrong sides of the black print to fit together at random. Join the long edge of one turquoise F and one diagonal stripe F. Repeat to make six F/F sets. Then join the edges of the diagonal stripe Fs (Diagram 13). Repeat to make three F/F/F/F sets.

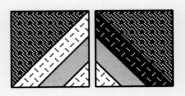

Diagram 13

Join the turquoise 5" x 3½", 1½" x 3½", 9½" x 3½" pieces and F/F/F/F sets into one strip (Diagram 14). Join the long edges of this strip and the turquoise 33" x 4½" strip. Join the opposite edge of the turquoise strip to the top of the design section. Then join the left edge of the whole design section to one long edge of the turquoise 13½" x 31½" piece.

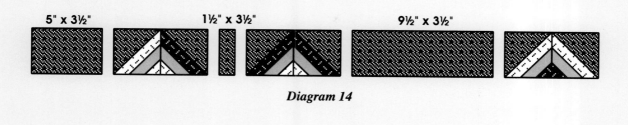

Diagram 14

6. **Add border.** Matching the centers, stitch the long border strips to the top and bottom edges of the quilt top. Then stitch the short border strips to the sides. Miter the corners.

7. **Complete quilt.** Mark quilting lines (Diagram 15). Layer the quilt backing (wrong side up), batting and the quilt top. Baste. Quilt all marked lines with aqua thread. Bind with gray bias tape. Miter the corners.

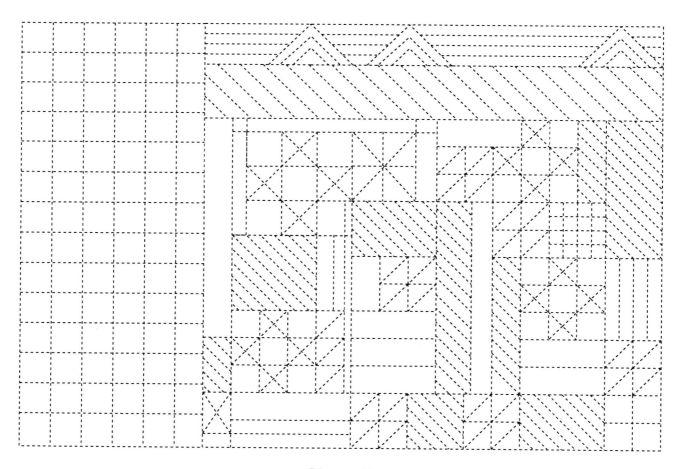

Diagram 15

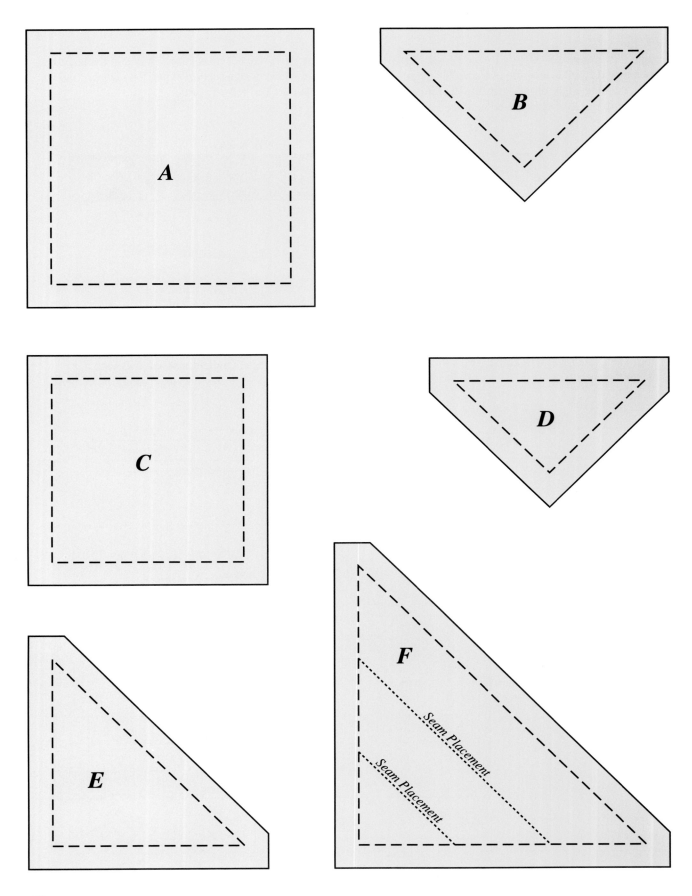

A

B

C

D

E

F

Seam Placement

Seam Placement

Mountain Memories

Mountain Memories

Build memories as you piece this colorful quilt, made with the help of a special template that ensures the perfect placement of the fabrics. While the materials call for eight different shades of each color of fabric, you needn't limit yourself to that number—it's the shading that's important. The result is a breathtaking quilt that is sure to stand the test of time.

Before you begin . . .

Each block consists of eight "rounds," which are indicated by lines on the template, and each round is made from fabric a shade lighter or darker than the previous round. Therefore, when choosing your eight (or more) different fabrics, be sure they range in shades from dark to light.

When stitching the rounds, always place the fabric strips on the *wrong* side of the template, and then stitch all of the seams on the *right* side of the template, through both the template and fabric. It's best to use a small stitch setting. Holding the template and fabric to the light is helpful for placement of the fabrics.

Always trim the seam allowances to ¼" after each round is complete. The center seams are close together, and therefore a little harder to stitch, but the rounds become easier to work as they get larger.

Finished size: 59" x 59"

Materials:

¼ yard total of eight different tan-print fabrics:
    Cut into 1¼"-wide strips

½ yard total of eight different gold-print fabrics:
    16 of Template C
    Eight of Template D
    Cut remaining fabric into 1¼"-wide strips

¾ yard of eight different green-print fabrics:
    Eight of Template G
    Eight of Template H
    Four of Template J
    Four of Template K
    Four of Template L
    16 of Template M
    Cut remaining fabric into 1¼"-wide strips

1 yard of eight different brown-print fabrics:
    Cut into 1¼"-wide strips

1¼ yards of eight different blue-print fabrics:
    Eight of Template C
    Four of Template E (short)
    Four of Template E (long)
    Eight of Template F
    Cut remaining fabric into 1¼"-wide strips

2¼ yards of black fabric:
    25 of Template A
    800 of Template B (To cut these quickly, cut 37 2"-wide strips of fabric. Fold them into 2" squares; cut. Fold each square in half diagonally; cut.)

3½ yards of navy-print fabric:
    Two 36" x 63" backing pieces

3 yards of cream-print fabric:
    Four 7½" x 63" border strips
    7 yards of 2"-wide bias for binding

One 60" x 60" piece of polyester fleece
5 yards of black bias tape
Thread for construction and quilting
Fabric glue or double-sided tape

Directions:

1. **Prepare 9" block templates.** Draw a template on graph paper for one 9" block (Diagram 1). Make 25 or more photocopies. (Because this block is larger than a standard 8½" x 11" sheet of paper, you may have to piece the graph paper carefully and use a copy machine which handles oversized sheets.) Trim each page to about ½" outside the edge of the block. Then, trace each line lightly on the wrong side of each template.

Arrange the templates in five rows of five blocks each. On the right side of one template, mark the color of each quarter of the block (Diagram 2). Then attach a small piece of fabric of the proper color to each line of the template, placing them so that they range from dark to light (the asterisks indicate placement of the darkest shade). Repeat for the remaining blocks (Diagram 3).

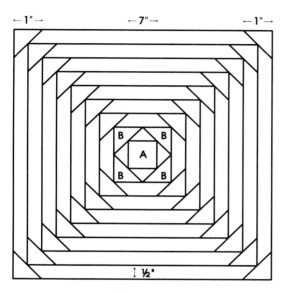

Diagram 1

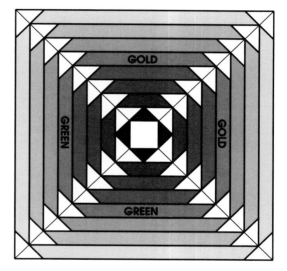

Diagram 2

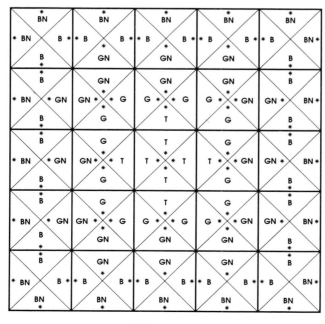

Diagram 3

B	=	Blue
BN	=	Brown
GN	=	Green
G	=	Gold
T	=	Tan

2. **Complete Round 1 of the center block.** Place one black A over the center of the wrong side of the center template, attaching with a small amount of water-soluble glue or a small piece of double-sided tape. From the darkest 1¼"-wide tan strip, cut four strips 2" long. Pin one strip to the wrong side of the template over the black A, aligning the raw edges and keeping the grain of the fabric parallel to the template lines. Stitch along the top line of the 1" square (Diagram 4). Repeat on the opposite edge of the black A. Press the strips open with the right side of the fabric showing.

Stitch the two remaining strips to the remaining edges of the 1" square (Diagram 5). Press both of the strips open.

Fold one black B under ¼" on the longest edge. Place the center of the folded edge over the strips at one corner of the black A, wrong side up, eyeing the placement. Pin to the wrong side of the template; unfold and stitch (Diagram 6).

Press the B open with the right side showing (Diagram 7). Repeat at the three remaining corners of the black A.

3. **Complete remaining rounds.** To begin the second round, cut four 1¼"-wide strips which are about ½" longer than the stitching lines. Pin one strip to the wrong side of the template over the previous round, aligning the raw edges and keeping the grain of the fabric parallel to the template lines. Stitch along the top line of the 2" square (Diagram 8). Repeat on the opposite edge of the 2" square. Press the strips open with the right side showing. Stitch the two remaining strips to the remaining edges of the 2" square. Press the strips open.

Pin four black Bs to the template (see Step 2), pinning them all at the same time. Stitch and press the pieces open. Repeat until all eight rounds are completed, cutting the strips about ½" longer than the corresponding stitching line. Repeat to make the remaining 24 blocks.

3. **Piece quilt top.** Remove all of the templates from the blocks. Carefully check each block and trim the outside edges as needed to measure 9½" x 9½". Join the blocks in rows following the color pattern (Diagram3).

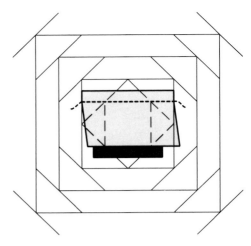

Diagram 4

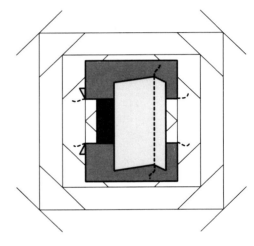

Diagram 5

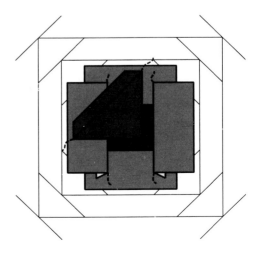

Diagram 6

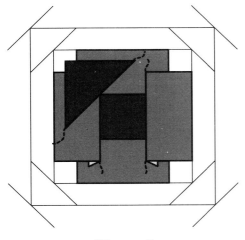

Diagram 7

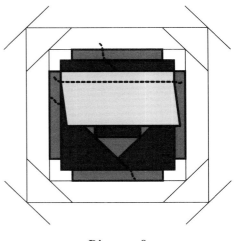

Diagram 8

4. **Add border.** Stitch one cream-print border strip to each side of the pieced quilt center, matching the centers. Miter the corners.

5. **Applique border.** Mark placement lines in the cream borders for Templates C through M (Diagram 9). Applique each template in alphabetical order, i.e., applique all Cs, then Ds, then Es, etc. Center and applique the black bias tape over each seam that joins the border and the quilt center, mitering the corners.

6. **Mark quilting lines.** Mark all quilting lines (Diagram 9). (The Quilting Pattern No. 1, No. 2 and No. 3 are on pages 76-77.)

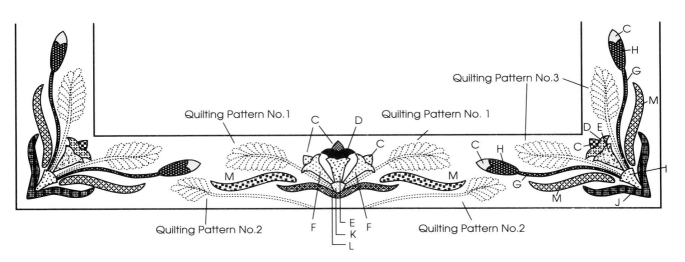

Diagram 9

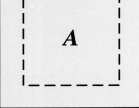

Diagram 10

7. Complete quilt. Stitch the two backing pieces together along one 63" edge. Layer the backing piece (wrong side up), fleece and quilt top. Baste. Trim to match quilt top edges. Quilt in-the-ditch of each block using thread that generally matches its colors (Diagram 10). Using cream thread, quilt all marked lines and in-the-ditch of each appliqued piece. Bind the quilt with the cream-print bias. Miter the corners. ❖

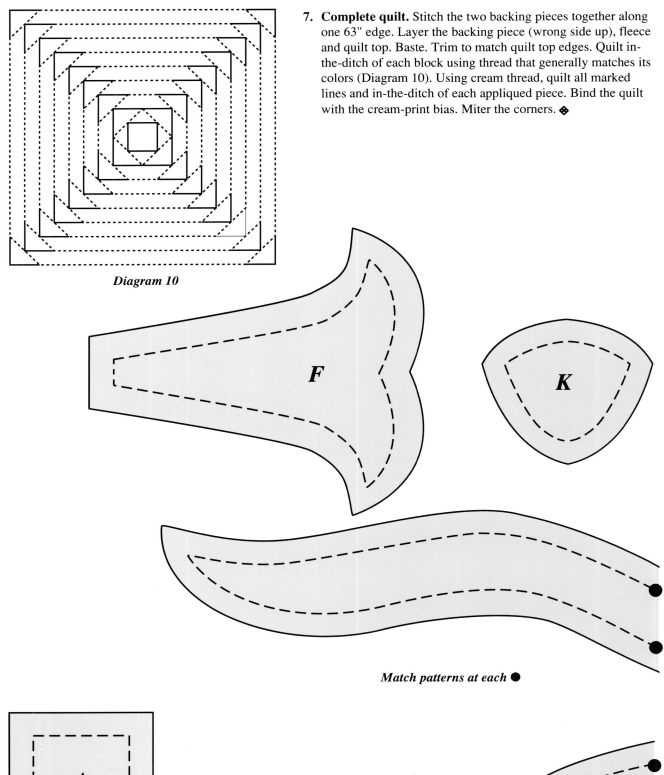

F

K

Match patterns at each ●

A

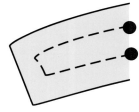

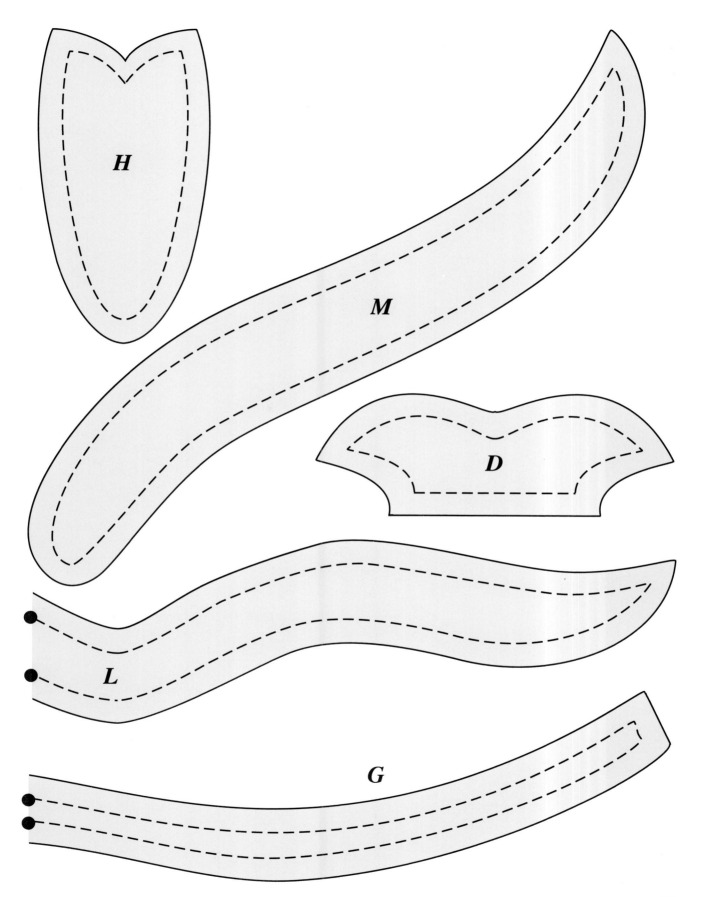

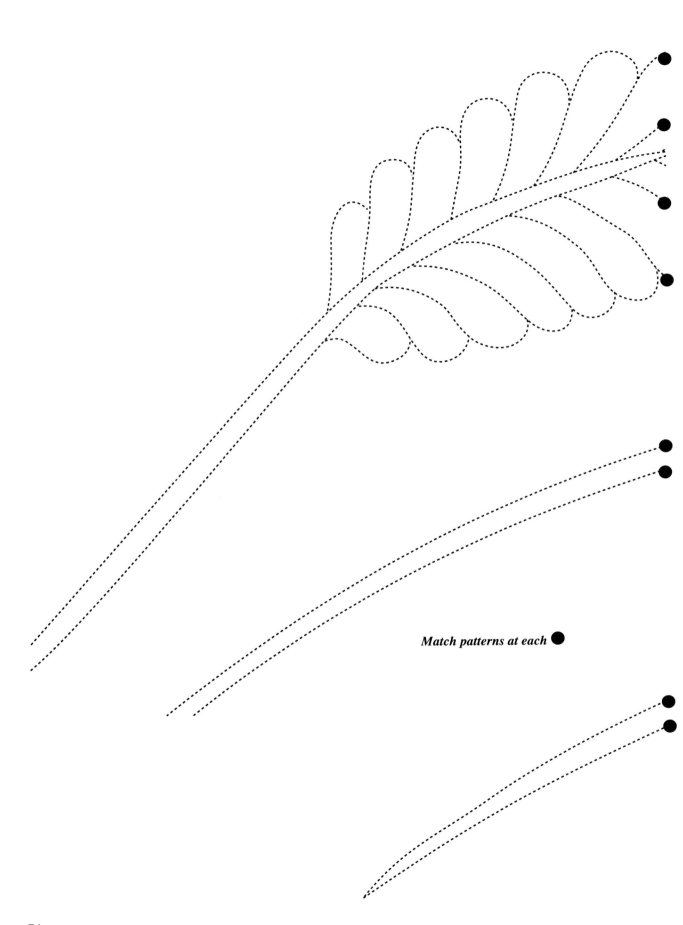

Match patterns at each ●

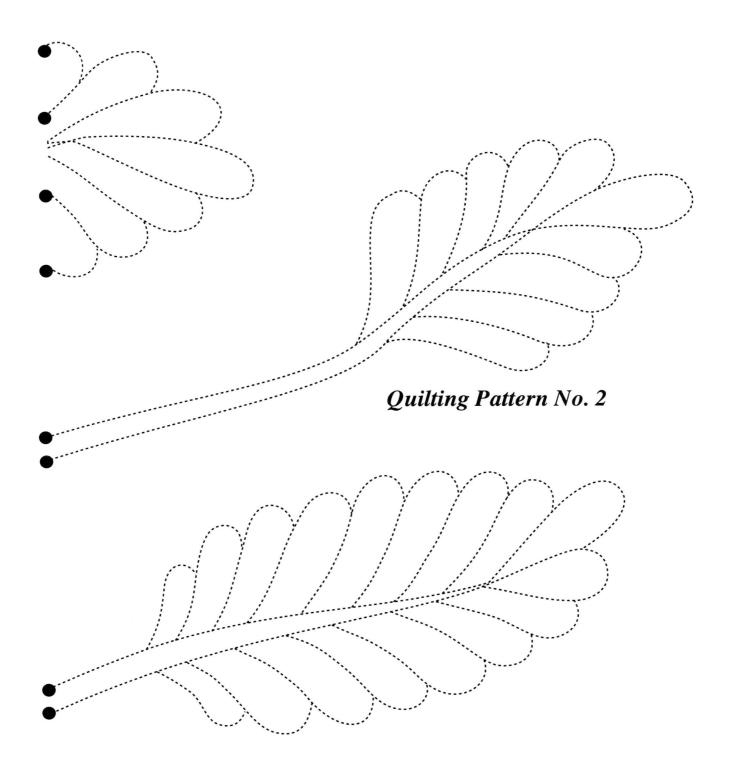

Quilting Pattern No. 2

Quilting Pattern No. 3

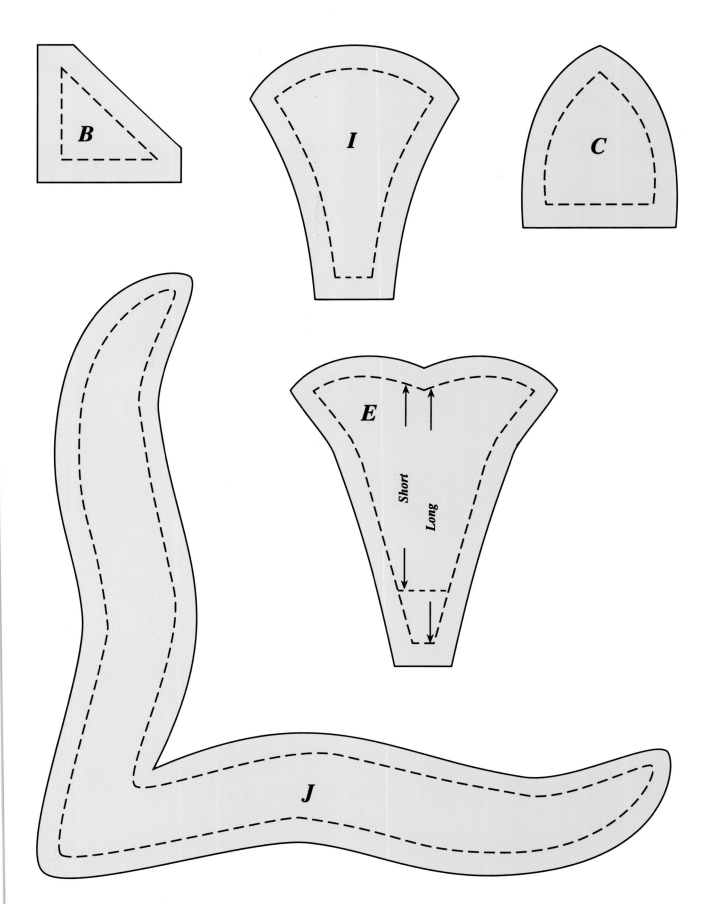

The Big Cover-Up

The Big Cover-Up

You'll love the durability of this uniquely decorative folding-chair cover. Piecing the blocks is a breeze, and with the help of a purchased pattern, you'll have a whole set stitched up in no time!

Finished size: 8" x 8"
(one block)

Note: The materials listed are based on the yardages used in our model. The measurements may vary depending upon your specific pattern and chair.

Materials:

5¾ yards of muslin:
  Cut ½ yard into 1½"-wide strips
  As many of Template A as needed (see Step 1)
  As many 8½" x 8½" squares as needed (see Step 1)
  One backing piece from pattern

1 yard of tan-stripe fabric:
  Cut ½ yard into 1½"-wide strips
  As many of Template A as needed (see Step 1)

2½ yards of batting
Purchased pattern for one folding chair cover

Directions:

1. **Determine number of blocks.** Mark an 8" x 8" grid on each purchased pattern piece, drawing the lines at a 45° angle to the straight of the fabric (Diagram 1). From the grid, measure the number of blocks you will need. (Half of that number will be design blocks, and the other half will be made from muslin.) Estimate the number of blocks needed for the smaller pattern pieces, such as the tie. Complete enough blocks for one pattern piece at a time.

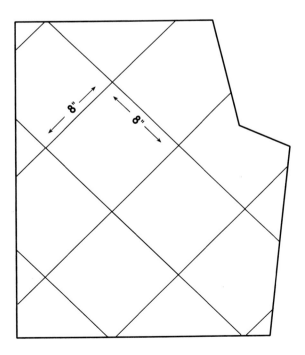

Diagram 1

2. Make design blocks. To make one design block, join the long edges of one 1½"-wide tan-stripe strip and one 1½"-wide muslin strip. Cut these into 1½"-wide segments. Join two segments to make one checkerboard (Diagram 2). Repeat to make eight checkerboards.

Join one muslin A to one tan-stripe A (Diagram 3). Repeat to make eight A/A sets. Then join two A/A sets and two checkerboard sets to make one square (Diagram 4). Repeat to make four squares. Join four squares to complete one design block (see schematic). Repeat to make as many design blocks as needed.

2. Complete quilted pattern pieces. Join the design blocks and the 8½" muslin squares in a checkerboard pattern to fit one pattern piece at a time. Cut one muslin backing piece and one piece of batting from the pattern piece. Layer the backing piece (wrong side up), batting and the design piece. Baste. Machine quilt in-the-ditch on all seams that join the design blocks to the muslin blocks. Also machine quilt in-the-ditch on the seams joining the A/A sets to the checkerboard sets. Repeat to make each piece called for in the purchased folding chair pattern. Cut the pieces out and complete the cover according to the purchased instructions. ◈

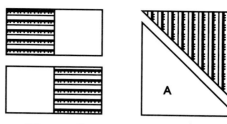

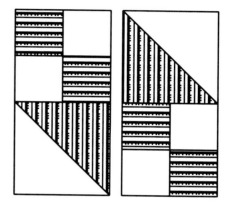

Diagram 2   *Diagram 3*

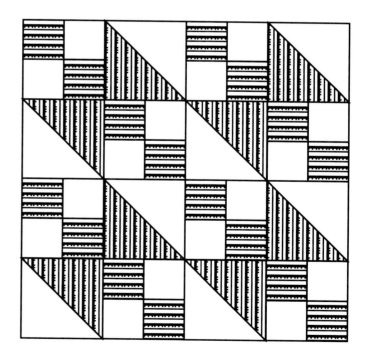

Diagram 4

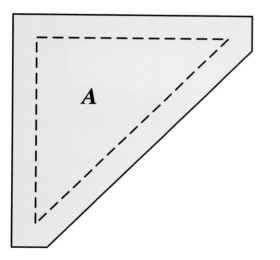

Block Schematic

Hidden Treasures

Who would guess that buried beneath this cleverly stencilled chair cushion is a hiding place? Our chair has a lift-up seat, but this idea can be used on many kinds of simple upholstered furniture pieces.

Directions:

1. **Piece background.** Measure the chair back and the seat at their widest points. Then, follow the steps below to calculate the number of Template As needed from each of the fabrics:

   1. Back: (Width measurement + 4) ÷ 2 = _____ (A)
   2. Back: (Length measurement + 4) ÷ 2 = _____ (B)
   3. Seat: (Width measurement + 4) ÷ 2 = _____ (C)
   4. Seat: (Length measurement + 4) ÷ 2 = _____ (D)
   5. (A + C) x (B + D) = _____ (E)
   6. E ÷ 5 = _____ (This is the number of Template As needed from each fabric.)

   Join the fabric As, placing the colors at random, in rows having the number of pieces calculated in A above. Then make B number of rows. Join the rows to make the back. Repeat to make the seat with C number of pieces wide by D number of rows.

2. **Stencil design.** Center and mark the shape of the back and the seat on the pieced fabric. Transfer the stencil patterns to the manila folder. Cut out the patterns with a craft knife. Stencil the flowers in groups as desired, mixing the paints as desired (see schematics). All of the leaves and the inside of each flower are painted light blue.

3. **Complete chair.** Upholster the back and seat to the chair. Glue the braid on the seams between the upholstered area and the chair. ❖

Finished size: Approximately 15" x 20" (two pieces)

Materials:

Solid fabrics in three shades of apricot: See Step 1

Solid fabrics in two shades of lavender: See Step 1

Thread for construction
Acrylic paints: lavender, light blue, medium blue, pink, and white
Manila folder for stencilling template
Craft knife
Stencil brush
Apricot upholstery braid
Wicker chair with a lift-up seat

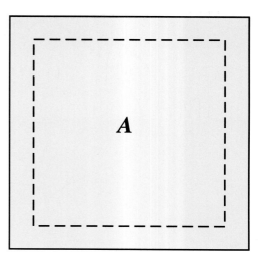

Seat Schematic

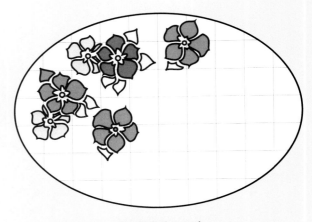

Back Schematic

Stencil Pattern No. 1

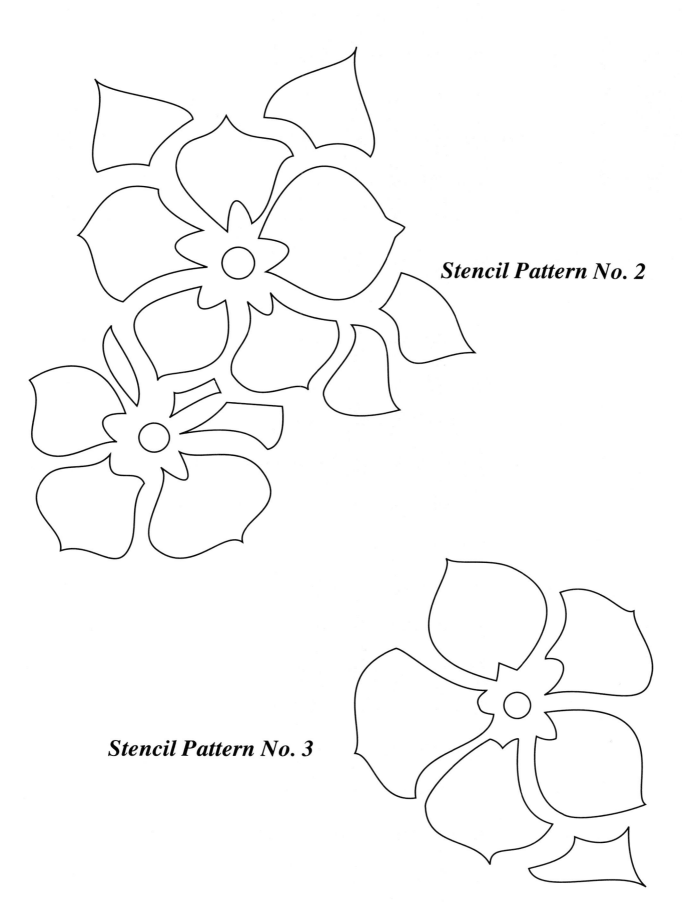

Stencil Pattern No. 2

Stencil Pattern No. 3

Santa Fe Ottoman

1. **Make center block.** Cut the following fabrics:
Four of Template A from cream print
One of Template B from red print
Four of Template C from red print

Assemble the center block (Diagram 1).

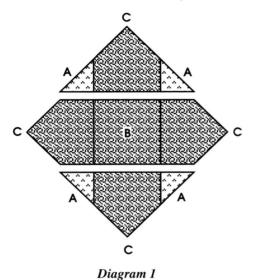

Diagram 1

2. **Make diagonal blocks.** Cut the following fabrics:
Eight of Template D from black
Four of Template F from cream print
24 of Template A from turquoise
12 of Template A from coral print
60 of Template A from tan
Eight of Template E from tan
16 of Template A from black
Four of Template G from tan

Join five tan As, one turquoise A and two black As, to make one corner set (Diagram 2). Repeat to make four corner sets.

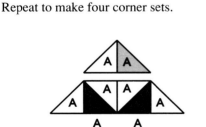

Diagram 2

Make another corner set, omitting one tan A (Diagram 3). Join this corner set, one cream-print F, two tan As, one coral-print A, one turquoise A and one tan E, to make one middle set (Diagram 3.) Repeat to make four middle sets.

Give new life to your old ottoman! This design, with its Native American elements, can be adapted to fit an ottoman of any size. Our instructions show how to make the top and four side panels, after which you will need to take the finished panels to a professional upholster to actually cover the ottoman. For the best quality, we recommend you consult the upholsterer prior to making the panels to determine the correct amounts of fabric to add or delete.

Finished size: Top Panel = 23"x 23"
One Side Panel = 23" x 13"

Materials:

2½ yards of tan fabric
⅜ yard of red-print fabric
¼ yard of black fabric
Scrap of turquoise fabric
Scrap of coral-print fabric
Scrap of cream-print fabric
2½ yards of medium corded piping
2¾ yards of polyester fleece
Tan thread for construction and quilting
2¾ yards of muslin
5½ yards of medium corded piping
One ottoman

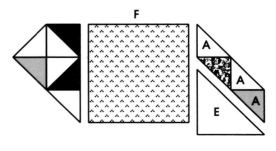

Diagram 3

Join four tan As, two coral-print As, three turquoise As, one tan E and one tan G, to make one bottom set (Diagram 4). Repeat to make four bottom sets.

Join one corner set, one middle set, one bottom set and two black Ds to make one diagonal block (Diagram 5). Repeat to make four diagonal blocks.

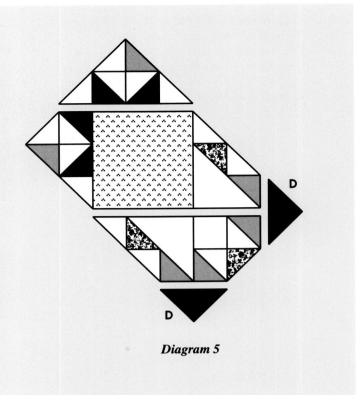

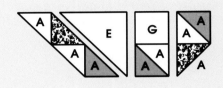

Diagram 4

Diagram 5

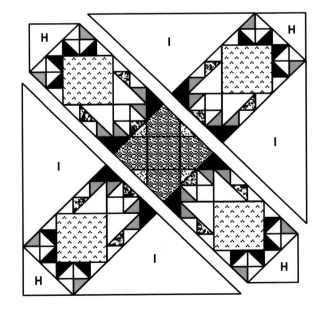

Diagram 6

3. **Make top design section.** Cut the following fabrics:
   Four of Template H from tan
   Four of Template I from tan

   Join the four diagonal blocks, four tan Is and four tan Hs, to make the top center section (Diagram 6).

4. **Make top panel.** Cut the following fabrics:
   Four 1" x 19" strips from tan
   Four 1" x 19" strips from red print
   56 of Template A from black
   24 of Template A from turquoise
   Four of Template G from coral print
   80 of Template A from tan
   Four 2" x 23" strips from tan (for a larger ottoman, add the necessary width to these strips)

   Join the long edges of one 1"-wide tan and one 1"-wide red-print strip to make one border set. Repeat to make four border sets. Join the tan sides of the border sets to the top center section, matching the centers and stitching to within ¼" of the corners; backstitch. Miter the corners.

Join two coral-print Gs, six turquoise As, 14 black As and 20 tan As to make the top sawtooth border (Diagram 7). Repeat to make the bottom sawtooth border. Repeat to make the two side sawtooth borders, omitting the coral-print Gs.

Join the side sawtooth borders to opposite edges of the center section. Then join the top and bottom sawtooth borders to the center section.

Join the 2"-wide tan strips to the center section, matching the centers and stitching to within ¼" of the corners; backstitch. Miter the corners.

Diagram 7

Top Panel Schematic

5. Make side design sections. Cut the following fabrics:

32 of Template J from cream print
32 of Template J from coral print
Four of Template G from coral print
Eight of Template J from turquoise
24 of Template A from turquoise
24 of Template D from black
Eight of Template C from red print
Four of Template B from red print
80 of Template A from tan
16 4½" x 1½" strips from tan
Four of Template G from tan
36 of Template D from tan
Eight of Template E from tan
24 1½" x 2½" strips from tan

Join three tan As to three turquoise As to make one triangle set (Diagram 8). Repeat to make eight triangle sets.

Diagram 8

Join one coral-print J to one cream-print J. Repeat to make 32 J/J sets. Join two J/J sets to make one checkerboard set (Diagram 9). Repeat to make 16 checkerboard sets.

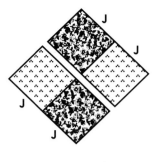

Diagram 9

Join one 1½" x 2½" tan piece to the long edge of one black D to make one black/tan set. Repeat to make 24 black/tan sets. Join four tan Ds to one turquoise J. Then join one 4½" x 1½" tan piece to each edge of this set (Diagram 10). Repeat to make eight tan/turquoise sets. Join one red-print B to two red-print Cs (Diagram 11). Repeat to make four B/C sets.

Assemble side design section (Diagram 12) (see "Setting In" in the General Instructions). Repeat to make four side design sections.

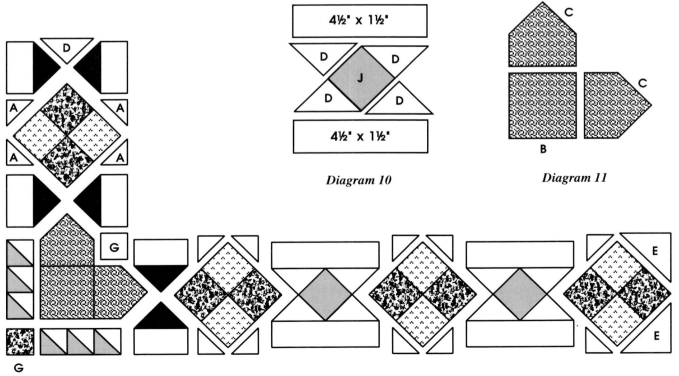

Diagram 10

Diagram 11

Diagram 12

6. Make side panels. Cut the following pieces from tan fabric (for a larger ottoman, add the necessary length and width to these pieces):

Eight 1½" x 4½" strips
Four 1½" x 13" strips
Four 18½" x 7½" pieces
Four 22½" x 2" strips

Join two 1½" x 4½" strips to the top edge and right ends of one side design section. Join one 18½" x 7½" piece to one side design section, stitching to, but not through, the inside corner of the design section and stopping. Begin again on the opposite side of the seam allowance to complete the seam. Join one 22½" x 2" strip to the bottom edge of the side design section, then join one 1½" x 13" piece to the left edge to make one side panel. Repeat to make four side panels.

7. Mark quilting lines. Mark all quilting lines (see the Top and Side Panel schematics). (The Top Quilting Pattern, Nos. 1 and 2 and the Side Quilting Pattern are on pages 92-93.)

8. Complete panels. Cut one tan piece the same size as each panel for the backing. Layer one tan backing piece (wrong side up), fleece and corresponding panel top. Baste. Using tan thread, quilt all marked lines. Also quilt in-the-ditch in all seams.

From red-print bias, make two 94" lengths of corded piping. Take corded piping and all panels to a professional upholsterer to cover the ottoman. ❖

Side Panel Schematic

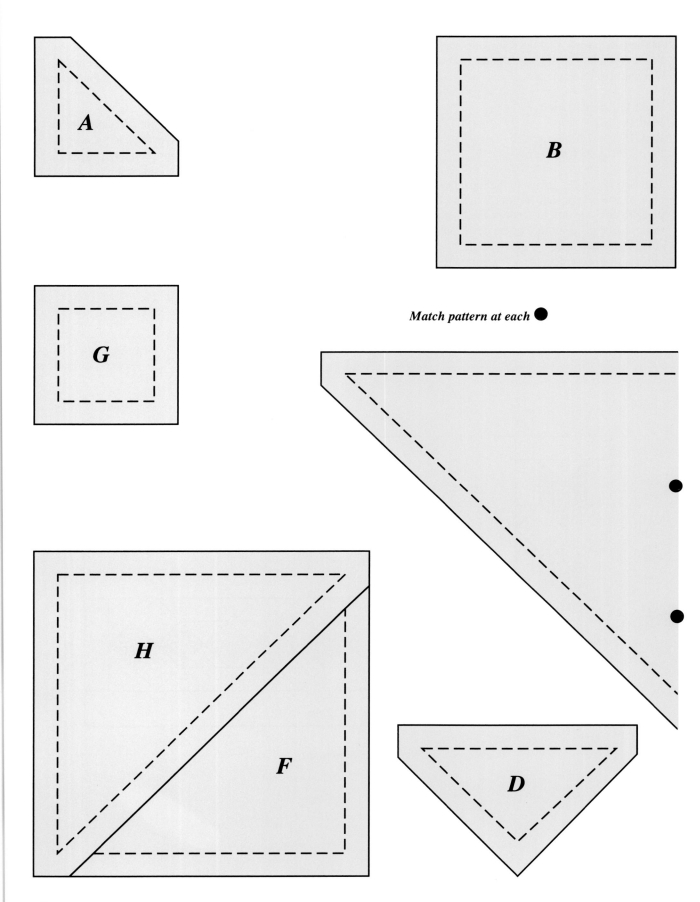

A

B

G

Match pattern at each ●

H

F

D

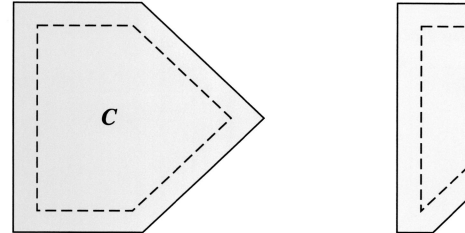

C

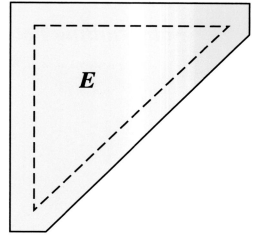

E

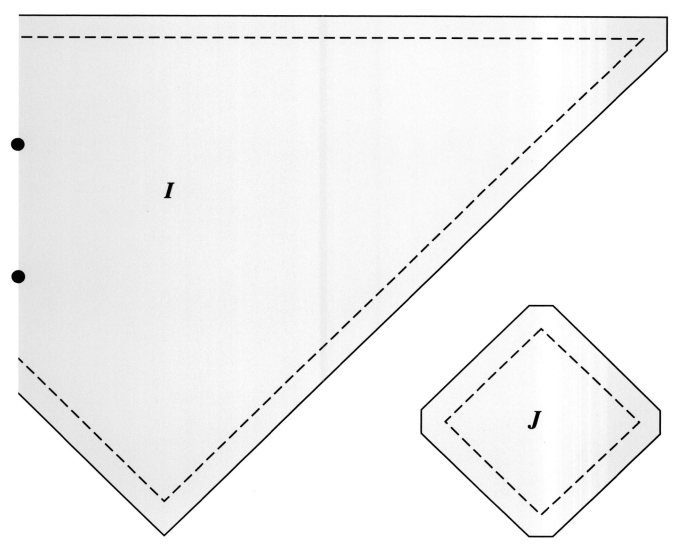

I

J

Side Quilting Pattern

Match patterns at each ●

Top Quilting Pattern, No. 1

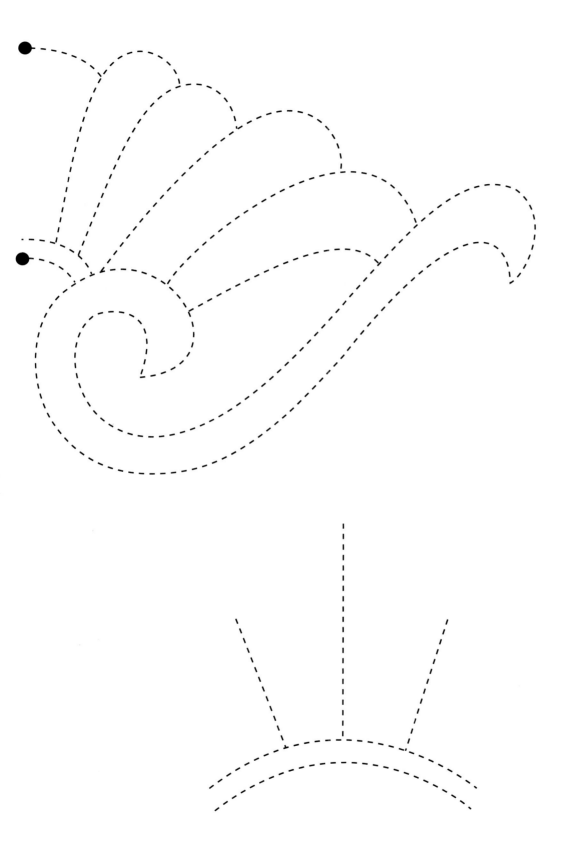

Top Quilting Pattern, No. 2

Diamonds 'n Dreams

Directions:

1. Make design section. Join three blue pindot As and three brown-print As (Diagram 1). Repeat to make two sets.

Join three blue pindot As and two brown-print As (Diagram 2).

Join the pieced sets and two tan pindot Ds (Diagram 3).

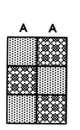 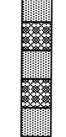

A   A

Diagram 1   *Diagram 2*   *Diagram 3*

Join the canvas Es to the pieced section to make the center section (Diagram 4).

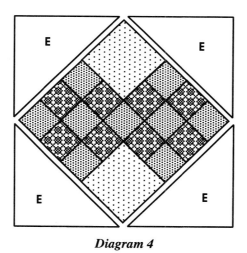

Diagram 4

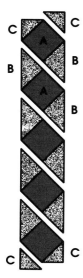

C   C

B   B

B

C   C

Diagram 5

Join five brown As, eight light-blue-print Bs and four light-blue Cs to make one side section (Diagram 5). Repeat to make two side sections. Join one dark-brown-print strip to one long edge of each side section. Join the diamond side of the side section to the center section to complete the design section (see the Pillow Sham Schematic).

Turn an ordinary set of sheets and pillowcases into an extraordinary ensemble with hand-fashioned border trims. Add a pair of homemade quilted canvas shams, and your boudoir will be adorned in style!

Pillow Sham

Finished size: 24" x30"

Materials for one pillow sham:

Scrap of blue pindot fabric:
  Nine of Template A

Scrap of brown-print fabric:
  Eight of Template A

Scrap of tan pindot fabric:
  Two of Template D

Scrap of brown fabric:
  Ten of Template A

⅛ yard of light-blue-print fabric:
  16 of Template B
  Eight of Template C

Scrap of dark-brown-print fabric:
  Two 1¾" x 11" strips

2¼ yards of lightweight canvas
  Four of Template E
  Two 7" x 24½" pieces
  Two 7" x 17½" pieces
  Two 24" x 33" backing pieces

⅝ yard of muslin:
  One 24½" x 30½" piece

⅝ yard of fleece
  One 24½" x 30½" piece

Cream thread for construction
Brown thread for quilting
One regular size bed pillow

2. **Piece pillow sham top.** Stitch one 7" x 17½" canvas piece to the top and bottom edges of the design section. Stitch one 7" x 24½" canvas piece to each side edge of the design section.

3. **Mark quilting lines.** (Diagram 6)

4. **Layer pillow sham top.** Layer the muslin, fleece and pillow sham top. Baste. Quilt all of the marked lines with brown thread.

5. **Complete pillow sham.** Fold each 24½" x 33" canvas piece to measure 24½" x 16½". Place the pillow sham top, right side up, on a flat surface.

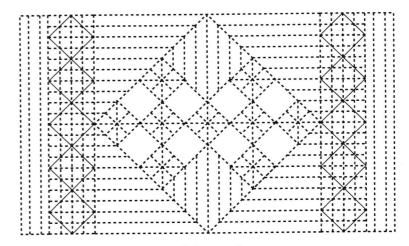

Diagram 6

Place the folded canvas piece over the pillow sham top, with the fold over the center of the sham and aligning all raw edges. Repeat with the second folded piece on the opposite side of the sham, overlapping the folded edges. Stitch all outside edges. Clip the corners. Turn. Mark 2" inside all edges. Topstitch through all of the layers. Insert the pillow.

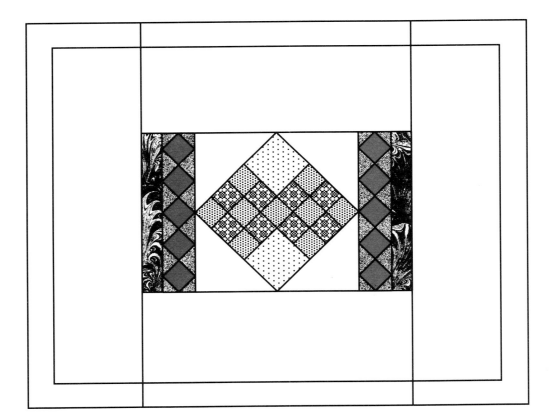

Pillow Sham Schematic

Bed Sheet Border

Finished size: 7" x 65"

Materials:

¼ yard of tan pindot fabric:
    16 of Template F
    16 of Template G

⅛ yard of blue pindot fabric:
    Four 2" x 32" strips

⅛ yard of brown-print fabric:
    Four 2" x 32" strips

¾ yards of blue fabric:
    67" of 1½"-wide bias

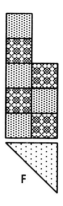

Diagram 7

Directions:

1. **Make diamond border.** Join the long edge of two 2"-wide brown-print strips and one 2"-wide blue pindot strip, alternating the colors. Cut these into 2" segments, making 16.

   Join the long edges of three 2"-wide blue pindot strips and two 2"-wide brown-print strips, alternating the colors. Cut these into 2"-wide segments, making 16.

   Join one three-piece segment to one five-piece segment. Then stitch the checkerboard pieces to one short edge of one tan pindot F to make one set (Diagram 7). Repeat to make 16 sets. Join the sets together to make the diamond border. (Diagram 8).

2. **Add tan and blue edgings.** Join two tan pindot Gs together (Diagram 9). Stitch the inside edge of one G to the checkerboard side of the diamond border, pivoting at the outside corner and stopping at the seam allowance of the inside corner. Join another tan pindot G to the end of the second G. Return to the opposite side of the seam allowance and stitch the G to the diamond border. Continue to add the Gs to the entire edge of the diamond border (Diagram 10).

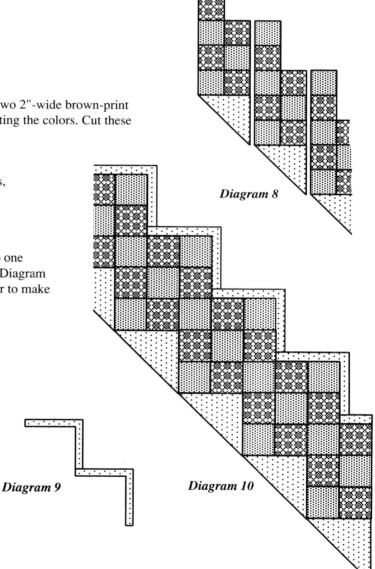

Diagram 8

Diagram 9

Diagram 10

3. **Complete bed sheet.** Position the blue bias strip over the sheet's top hem; stitch the top long edge to the sheet with right sides together. Unfold and press with the raw edge of the bias strip away from the top of the sheet. Match the long raw edge of the blue bias strip with the diamond border; stitch through all layers. Unfold and press; baste to the sheet. Turn the tan pindot Gs under ¼", clipping inside the corners; slipstitch to the sheet. Turn the diamond border ends under ¼"; slipstitch to the sheet.

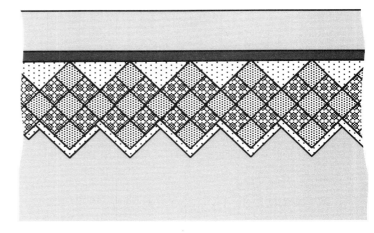

Bed Sheet Schematic

Pillow Case Border

Finished size: 3" x 40"

Materials (for one standard pillow case):

⅛ yard of brown fabric:
   18 of Template A

⅛ yard of blue-print fabric:
   36 of Template B

½ yard of dark-brown fabric:
   42" of 1½"-wide bias

One purchased standard pillowcase

Directions:

1 **Make diamond border.** Join two blue-print Bs to the opposite edges of one brown A (Diagram 12). Repeat to make 18 sets. Then join the sets in a row (Diagram 13).

2. **Complete pillow case.** Position the dark-brown bias strip over the hem of the pillow case; stitch one long edge to the pillow case with right sides together. Unfold and press with the raw edge of the bias strip away from the hemmed edge. Stitch the raw edges of the bias strip and one long edge of the diamond border with right sides together. Unfold and press. Baste the border to the pillow case. Turn the opposite edge of the diamond border under ¼"; slipstitch to the pillow case. Turn the ends of the diamond border under ¼"; slipstitch to the pillow case. ❖

Diagram 12

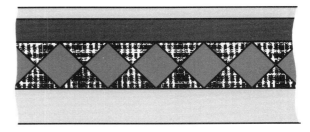

Diagram 13

Pillow Case Schematic

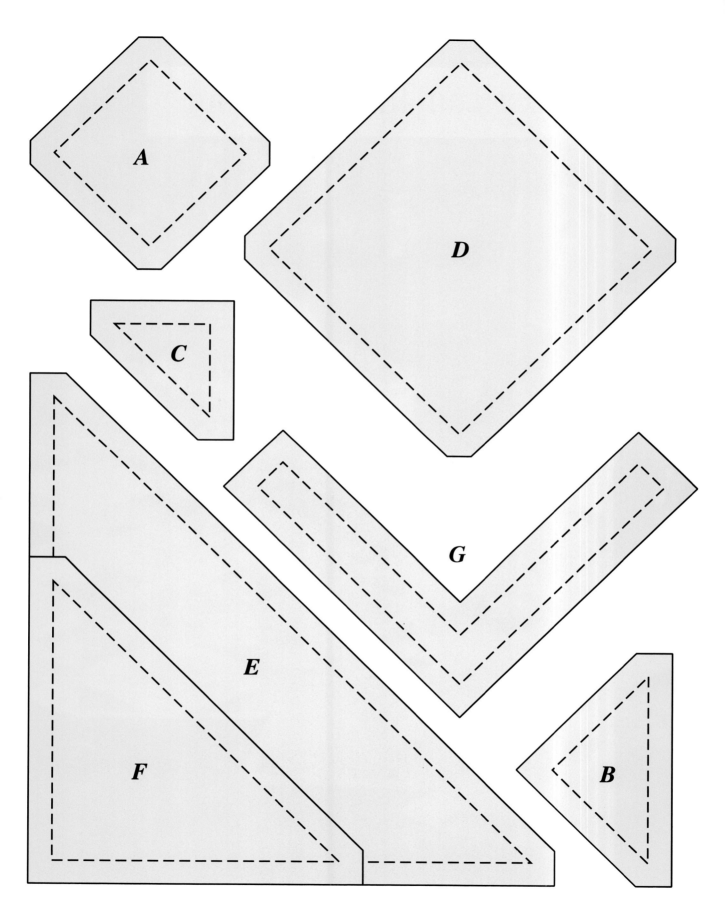

Early American Table Setting

Directions:

1. **Make red blocks.** Join four red Bs to one muslin A to make one red block (Diagram 1). Repeat to make 20 red blocks.

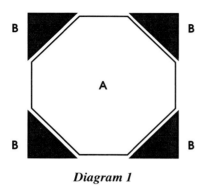

Diagram 1

2. **Make blue blocks.** Join one blue-stripe B and one muslin B (Diagram 2). Repeat to make 62 B/B sets. Join the B/B sets, four blue-stripe Cs and one muslin C to make one blue block (Diagram 3). Repeat to make 11 blue blocks.

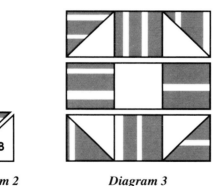

Diagram 2   *Diagram 3*

3. **Make half-blocks.** Join one blue-stripe D and one muslin D (Diagram 4). Repeat to make 36 D/D sets.

Join two D/D sets, one B/B set, two blue-stripe Cs and one muslin B to make one half-block (Diagram 5). Repeat to make 18 half-blocks.

Diagram 4   *Diagram 5*

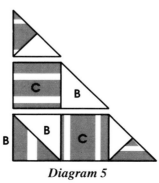

Table Runner

As the family gathers to dine, this table setting will blanket them in a rustic warmth found in traditional country homes. The set includes a table runner, place mat, napkin and napkin ring.

Finished size: 96" x 20"

Materials:

3 yards of muslin:
   20 of Template A
   80 of Template B
   11 of Template C
   36 of Template D
   One 20" x 96" backing piece
   5¾ yards of 1½"-wide bias binding strips

1¾ yards of blue-stripe fabric:
   62 of Template B
   80 of Template C
   36 Template D

1 yard of red fabric:
   80 of Template B

2⅝ yards polyester fleece
   One 20" x 96" piece

Cream thread for construction and quilting

4. Make table runner top. Join the blocks to make 11 rows as follows (Diagram 6):

Rows 1 and 11:   one blue block, one red block and one half-block

Rows 2 and 10:   one red block, one blue block, one red block and one half-block

Rows 3-9:   one half-block, one red block, one blue block, one red block, and one half-block

Join the rows to complete the table runner top.

5. Mark quilting lines. Draw three horizontal lines ½" apart 1½" from one straight edge of table runner. Draw three more lines 1½" from the first set. Repeat until table runner is filled with sets of three horizontal lines (see Table Runner Schematic).

6. Complete table runner. Layer the backing (wrong side up), fleece and table runner top. Trim to match the table runner top. Baste. Quilt on all marked lines with cream thread. Bind the edges with the muslin bias. Miter the corners.

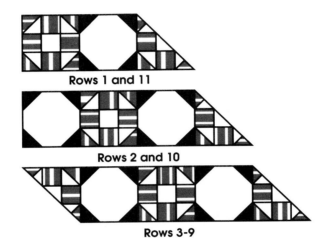

Rows 1 and 11

Rows 2 and 10

Rows 3-9

Diagram 6

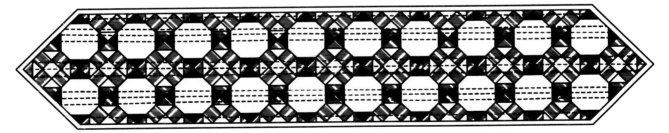

Table Runner Schematic

Napkin

Finished size: 15" x 15" (one napkin)

Materials for one red and one blue napkin:

1½ yards of muslin
    One of Template A
    Two of Template B
    Two of Template D
    Four 15" x 15" pieces
    3¾ yards of 1¼"-wide bias strips for
       binding

⅛ yard of blue-stripe fabric
    One Template B
    Two Template C
    Two Template D

⅛ yard of red fabric
    Four Template B

Scraps of polyester fleece
    One 6" x 6" piece

Cream thread for construction
and quilting

Directions:

1. **Make design section of blue napkin.**
Make one half block; see Step 3 of the
table runner. Mark one quilting line ¾"
from and parallel to the long edge of the
half-block. Then draw one parallel line
½" on each side of the first line.

2. **Make design section of red napkin.**
Make one red block; see Step 1 of the
table runner. Cut the block in half from
corner to corner. Mark one quilting line in
the center of one of the triangles perpen-
dicular to the long edge. Mark one
quilting line ½" from and parallel to the
first line on each side. Mark an additional
set of quilting lines 1" from and parallel to
each side of the first set. (Use the remaining triangle to make another napkin.)

3. **Complete napkin.** Trim the corner from
one 15" x 15" muslin piece (Diagram 7).
Then stitch the design section to the cut
corner. Cut the 6" x 6" piece of fleece in
half from corner to corner. Layer the uncut
muslin piece (wrong side up), fleece and
design piece. Baste. Quilt all marked lines
using cream thread. Bind all edges of the
napkin with muslin bias. Miter the corners.
Repeat for second napkin.

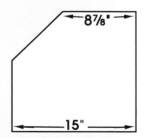

Diagram 7

Napkin Ring

Finished size 8½" x 3" (one napkin ring)

Materials for one red and one blue napkin ring:

1½ yards of muslin:
    Two of Template B
    One of Template C
    One 6½" x 3" piece
    Two 8½" x 3" backing pieces
    1⅛ yards of 1¼"-wide bias strips
    for binding

Scrap of blue-stripe fabric:
    Six of Template B

Scrap of red fabric
    Two of Template B

Scrap of polyester fleece

Directions:

1. **Make blue design section.** Join six blue-stripe Bs, two muslin Bs and one muslin C. Mark all of the quilting lines (see schematic).

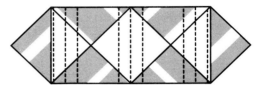

Blue Napkin Ring Schematic

2. **Make red design section.** Join the long edge of one red B to each 3" end of the 6½" x 3" muslin piece. Mark three quilting lines, ½" apart and parallel to the long edges in the center of the section (see schematic).

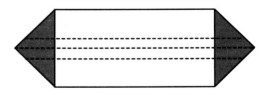

Red Napkin Ring Schematic

3. **Complete napkin ring.** Layer one backing piece and one design section. Trim the backing piece to match the design section. Quilt all marked lines using cream thread. Bind the napkin ring with muslin bias. Slipstitch the points of the napking ring together (see photo). Repeat for the second napkin ring.

Place Mat

Directions:

1. **Make place mat top.** Make four red blocks; see Step 1 of the table runner. Make one blue block; see Step 2 of the table runner. Make four half-blocks; see Step 3 of the table runner. Make three rows from the blocks (Diagram 10). Join the rows together.

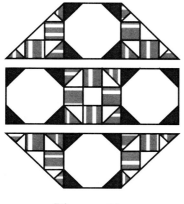

Diagram 10

2. **Mark quilting lines.** Draw three horizontal lines ½" apart 1½" from one straight edge of place mat. Draw three more lines 1½" from first set. Repeat until place mat top is filled with sets of three horizontal lines (Diagram 11).

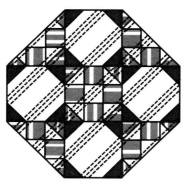

Diagram 11

3. **Complete place mat.** Layer the backing (wrong side up), fleece and place mat top. Baste. Trim to fit the place mat top. Quilt on all marked lines with cream thread. Bind the place mat with muslin bias. ❖

Finished size: 18" x 18"

Materials:

¾ yard of muslin :
   Four of Template A
   12 of Template B
   One of Template C
   Eight of Template D
   One 18½" x 18½" square
   for backing
   1⅝ yards of 1½"-wide bias
   strips for binding

⅛ yard of red fabric:
   16 of Template B

¼ yard of blue-stripe fabric:
   Eight of Template B
   12 of Template C
   Eight of Template D

¾ yard of polyester fleece:
   One 18½" x 18½" piece

Cream thread for construction
and quilting

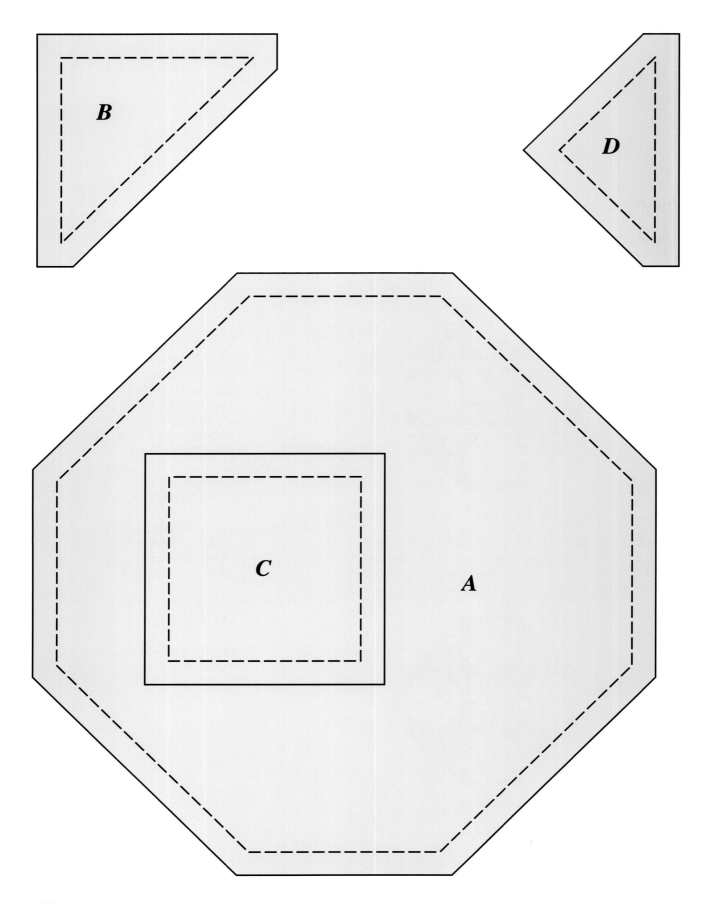

Tiny Tuffet

Any little Miss Muffet would be proud to sit on this little tuffet, complete with a spider to sit down beside her.

Finished size: 10½" x 16"

Materials:

½ yard of muslin
Scraps of assorted burgundy, pink, and green silk fabrics
Scraps of assorted burgundy, pink, and green cotton fabrics
Small pieces of satin and grosgrain ribbons
Two antique buttons
Embroidery floss in matching colors
Braid to cover edge of upholstered area
Staple gun and staples
Glue
One purchased footstool

Directions:

1. **Prepare design piece.** Cut the muslin 2" larger on all edges than the footstool top. Crazy-quilt the cottons and silks to the muslin at random. Embellish the seams with various embroidery stitches. Quilt on the print fabrics, using the print pattern as a guide. Applique small lengths of ribbon where desired. Attach the buttons where desired.

2. **Finish footstool.** Upholster the crazy-quilted design piece to the top of the footstool. Cover the edge with the decorative braid. ❖

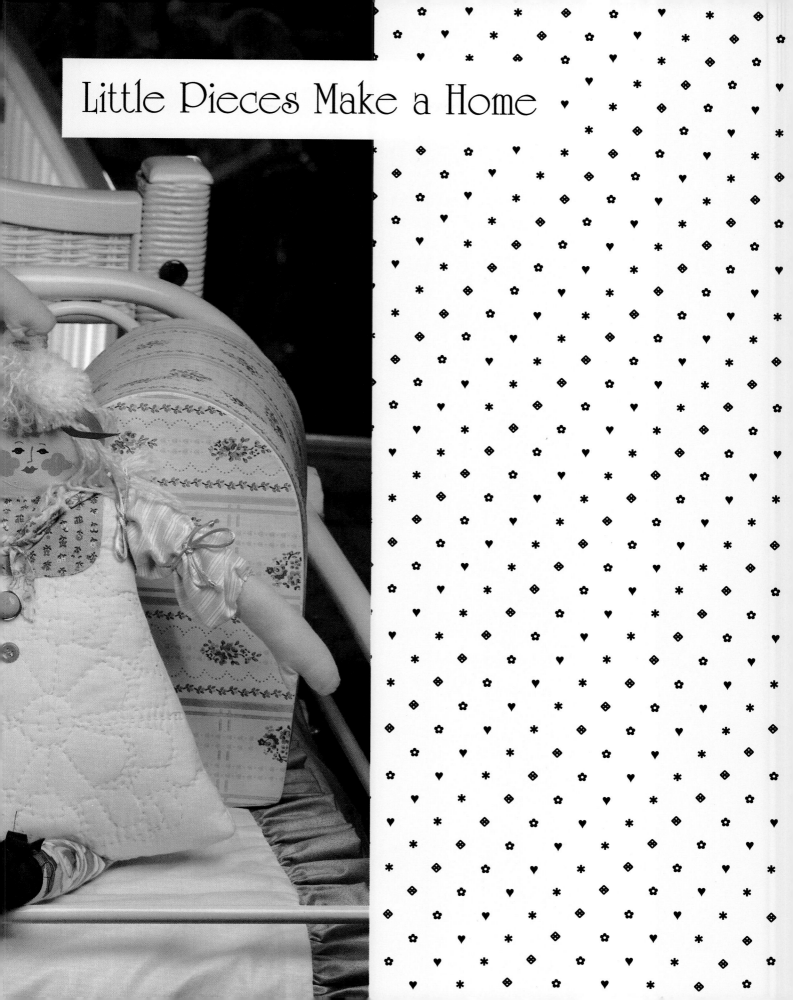

Little Pieces Make a Home

Three on a Whim!

Our designer lends a whimsical new idea to an old rag doll tradition, combining remnants of an old quilt, fashionable prints, and the lopsided placement of trims and limbs.

Finished size: 20" long (one doll)

Materials for one doll:

One old quilt:
    Two 11" x 13" pieces for body

Scrap of cream fabric:
    Two HEAD pieces

Scrap of pink fabric:
    Four ARMs

Scrap of black fabric:
    Two SHOEs
    Two 17" x ½" strips

Scrap of cream-print fabric:
    Two 4½" x 8" pieces for legs

Scrap of cream-stripe fabric:
    Two 4½" x 6" pieces for sleeves

Scrap of green-print fabric:
    One SCARF

½ yard of ribbon for hair (see photo)
1¼ yards of small pink rayon cording
One skein of cream yarn
Acrylic paints (see Step 4)
Three assorted buttons
Stuffing

Directions:

1. **Make arms and legs.** Join two ARM pieces, leaving an opening. Clip the seam allowance at the thumb. Turn. Stuff the arm firmly to within ½" of the opening. Repeat for the second arm.

   To make the legs, fold one cream-print leg piece to measure 2¼"-wide. Stitch the long edge, then round-off one end, leaving the opposite end open. Stuff firmly to within ½" of the opening. Repeat for the second leg.

2. **Make body.** Baste the arms and legs to the right side of the body front with right sides together (see pattern). Stitch the body front to the back, leaving an opening at the head and securing the arms and legs in the seams. Turn. Stuff firmly. Insert the HEAD in the opening of the body. Slipstitch the seams closed to the edge of the head; slipstitch the head securely to the body.

3. **Make clothing.** To make the sleeves, stitch the 6" edges of one cream-stripe sleeve piece to measure 2¼" x 6". Turn each open end under ¼" and stitch. Turn. Mark half-way between each end and sew running stitches around both ends on the center mark. Slide the sleeve over the doll arm (see photo) and gather to fit; secure the threads. Cut four pieces of cording. Tie over the sleeve (see photo). Repeat for second sleeve.

   To make the shoes, stitch the center back seam of one SHOE. Slide onto the foot. Fold the front and back edges of the shoe piece to meet at the bottom of the foot; slipstitch. Fold the right and left edges to meet at the center bottom of the foot like a paper bag; slipstitch. Whipstitch the top and oval edges of the shoe to the doll leg. Tie and criss-cross the 17"-long black strips around the top of the shoe in ballerina fashion. Repeat for the opposite shoe.

To make the collar, place the COLLAR on the doll. Slipstitch the center back loosely to the doll body. Tie the SCARF over the collar.

4. **Embellish doll**. Mark a 1⅞"-wide circle on the doll's face. Paint the circle with pink paint. Transfer the face details to the painted area (Diagram 1). Paint dark-pink cheeks, red lips, dark-blue eyes, and a brown nose and eyebrows.

Cut the cream yarn into 9" lengths and slipstitch to the doll's head, arranging as desired. Add ribbons to the hair as desired (see photo). Sew buttons to the body front as desired. ❖

Diagram 1

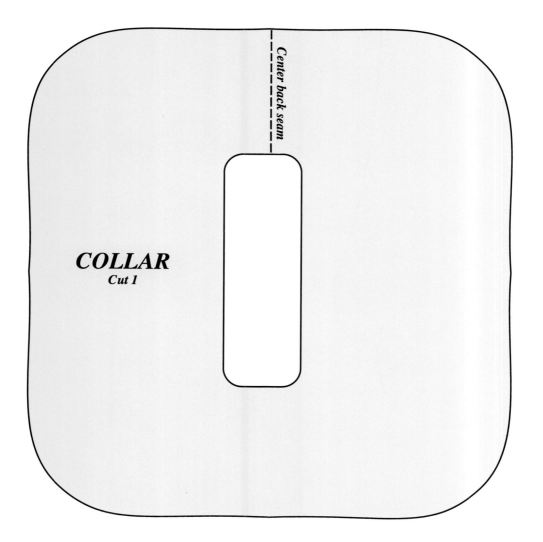

Center back seam

COLLAR
Cut 1

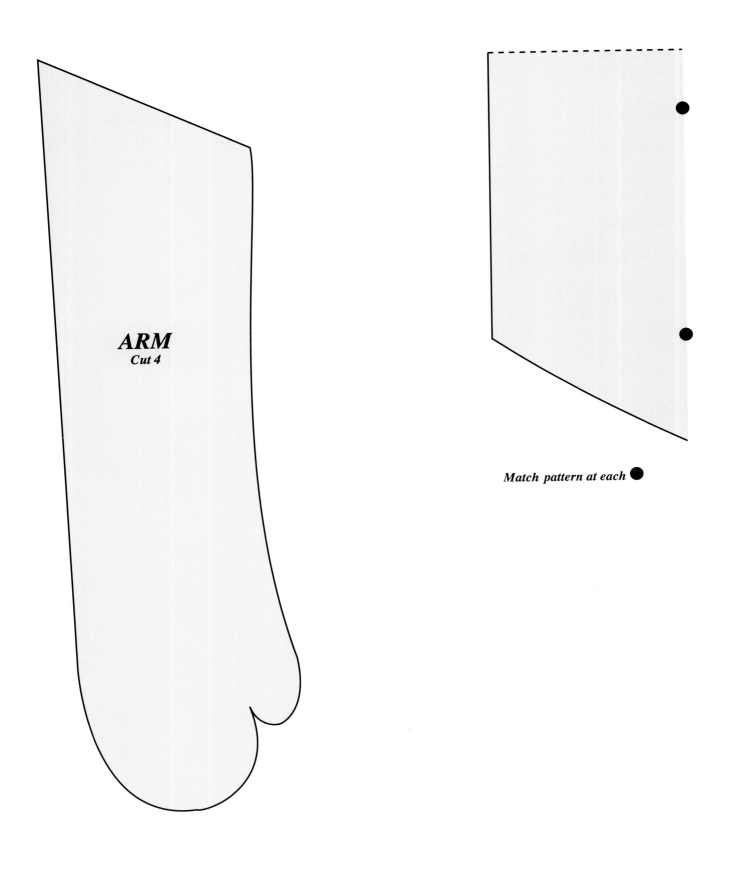

ARM
Cut 4

Match pattern at each ●

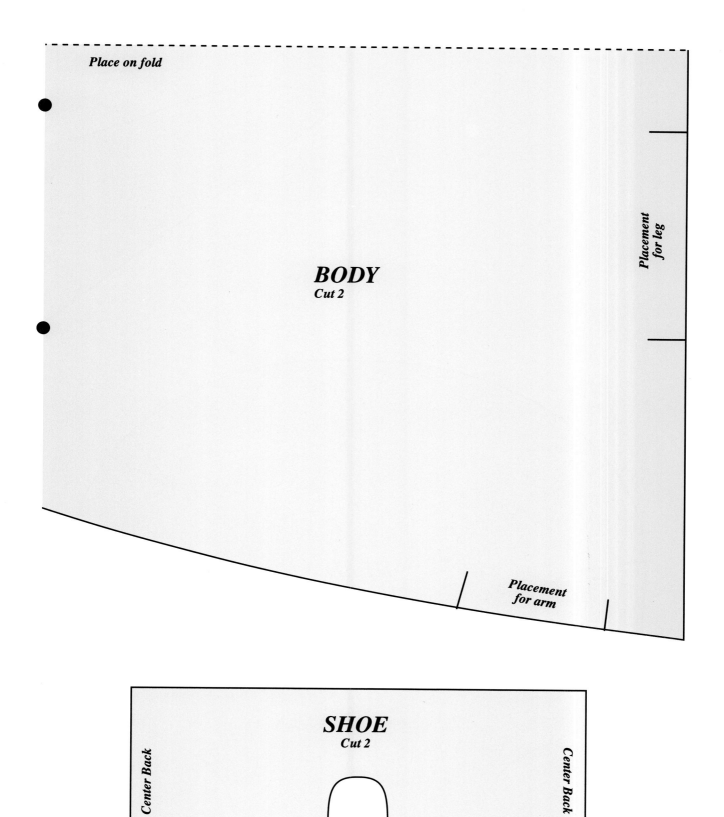

Place on fold

BODY
Cut 2

Placement for leg

Placement for arm

SHOE
Cut 2

Center Back

Center Back

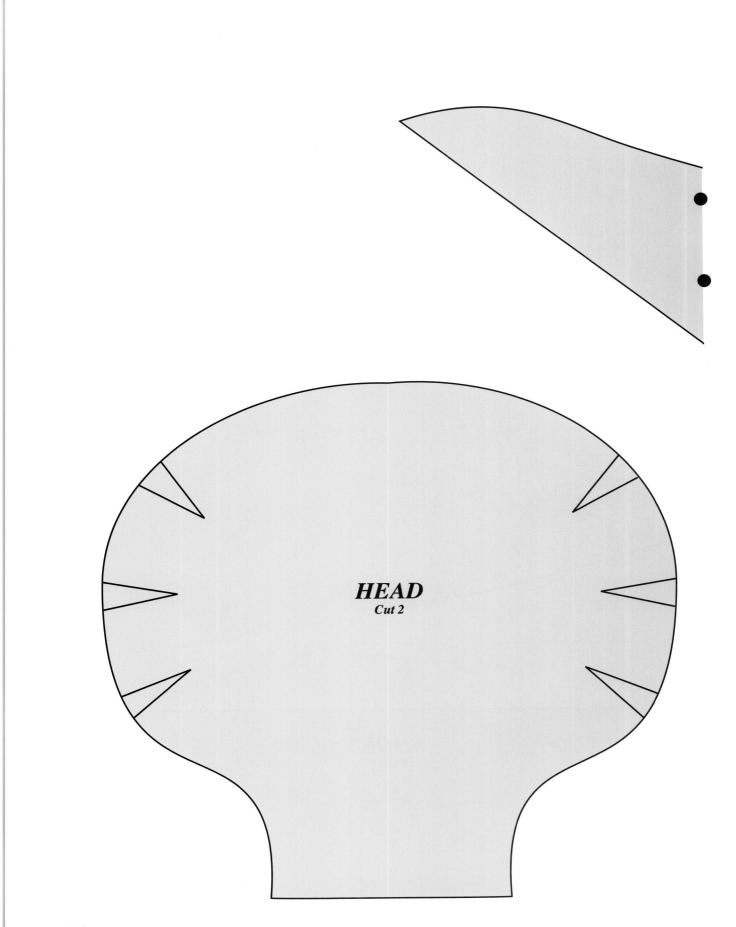

HEAD
Cut 2

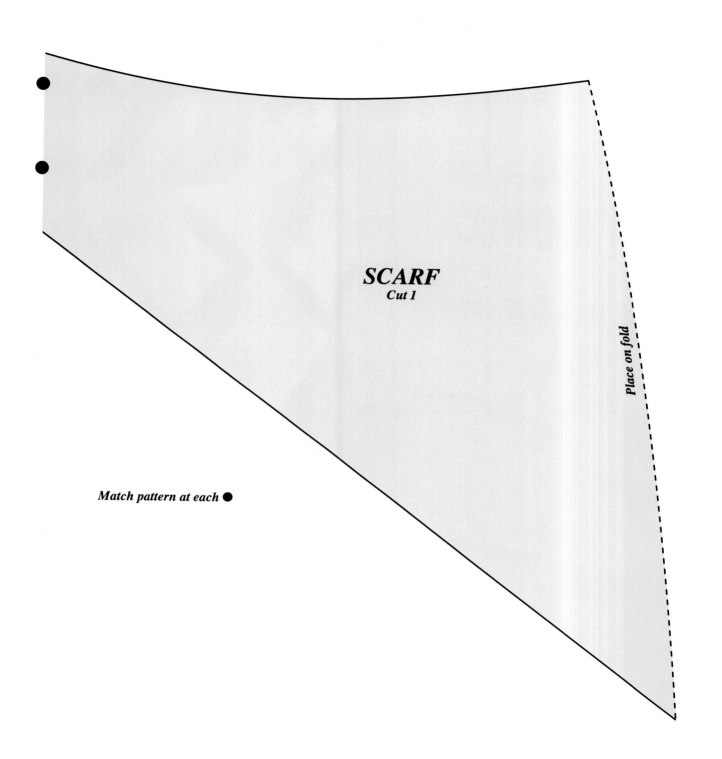

SCARF
Cut 1

Place on fold

Match pattern at each ●

Carnival Winds

Directions:

1. **Make diamond section**. Join four
   different 1½" x 5⅛" pieces to one
   yellow C. Stitch the first piece to
   one edge of the yellow C, stopping
   ½" from the adjacent edge. Then
   join the second piece, stitching over
   the end of the first (Diagram 1).

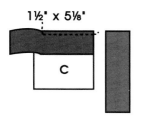

Diagram 1

Continue to work clockwise, joining
the third and fourth pieces. Return to
the first piece and complete the seam.
Repeat to make five diamond sets
using the two remaining yellow Cs
and the two white Cs, changing the
color combinations and placement of
the 1½" x 5⅛" pieces.

Join one white D to the upper left and
one orange D to the upper right edges
of the diamond. Join one orange E and
one white E to the bottom edges
(Diagram 2). Repeat for each diamond.

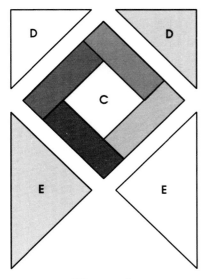

Diagram 2

*On any given day, from July
through Labor Day, a windsock
like this might be seen by
passersby, adding a carnival-like
charm to the ordinary.*

Finished size: 40" circumference, 12" diameter, 36" long

Materials:

⅝ yard of yellow fabric:
   Four of Template A
   Six of Template B
   Three of Template C
   Two of Template F
   Ten of Template G
   Two 3¼" x 19" strips

⅞ yard of orange fabric:
   Four of Template A
   Five of Template D
   Five of Template E
   One of Template F
   One 3¼" x 19" piece
   Two 4¼" x 28½" pieces

⅝ yard of melon fabric:
   Six of Template B
   One 3" x 40½" piece
   Two 3¼" x 19" pieces
   Two 4¼" x 28½" pieces

¼ yard of rose fabric:
   Five 1½" x 5⅛" pieces
   Three 3¼" x 19" pieces

½ yard of red fabric:
   Four 4¼" x 28½" pieces

¼ yard of green fabric:
   Four of Template A
   Five 1½" x 5⅛" pieces

⅝ yard of blue fabric:
   Four of Template B
   One of Template F
   Five 1½" x 5⅛" pieces
   One 3¼" x 19" piece

¼ yard of purple fabric:
   Five 1½" x 5⅛" pieces
   Two 4¼" x 28½" pieces

1½ yards of white fabric:
   Four of Template B
   Two of Template C
   Five of Template D
   Five of Template E
   One of Template F
   One 3¼" x 19" piece
   One 7¼" x 40½" piece
   One 12" x 40½" piece
   40" of 3"-wide bias strips

   One 12" diameter macrame
hoop
2 yards of matching cording

Join two yellow Gs on two sides (Diagram 3). Clip the corner. Turn. Repeat to make five sets. Pin to the orange Es 1¼" from the top corner on the long edge (Diagram 4).

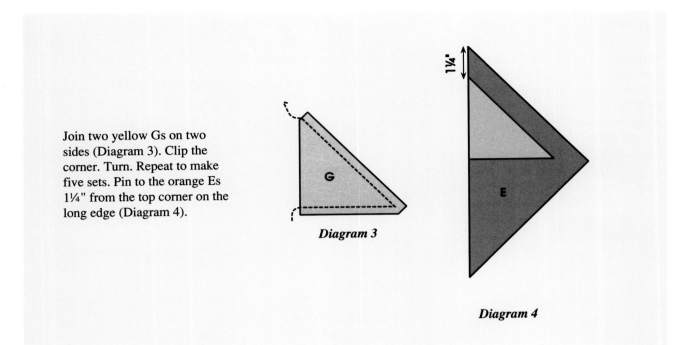

Diagram 3

Diagram 4

Join the long edges of the diamond sets to make five in one long row with four yellow Gs secured in the seams. Pin the fifth yellow G to the left edge; press. Using the completed diamond section as a pattern, cut the lining from the 12" x 40½" white piece. Join on the lower zigzag edge. Clip the corners and seam allowances. Turn. Then, with the diamond section and lining unfolded, join the ends of the diamond section and lining to make one large circle, securing the fifth G in the seam. Set aside.

2. **Make diagonal section.** Stitch the long edges of the Bs together in a random color pattern. Join the edges of the first and last Bs to make one large circle. Stitch one 3" x 40½" melon piece to the top edge of the diagonal section. Join the ends to make one large circle. Set the diagonal section aside.

3. **Make streamers.** Match two 4¼" x 28½" melon pieces. Using Template G, mark the point on one narrow end. Stitch both edges and marked point. Trim the seam allowance of the point to ¼". Clip the corners. Turn. Repeat to make five large streamers made of different colors.

Place Template F on one narrow end of a 3¼" x 19" melon piece. Mark the long diagonal line. Join one orange F to the melon piece on the diagonal line. Trim all layers to ¼" seam allowance. Match the melon/orange F piece to one 3¼" x 19" orange piece. Stitch both long edges and the point. Trim the seam allowance of the point to ¼". Clip the corners. Turn. Repeat to make two rose/yellow F/yellow streamers, one melon/blue F/blue streamer, and one rose/white F/white streamer.

4. **Assemble windsock.** Pin the top edge of one short streamer to the top edge of the diamond section, centering the streamer. Then pin the long streamer, matching top edges, behind the right half of the diamond and overlapping the short streamer (see schematic). Repeat behind each diamond.

Slide the diagonal section over the right side of the diamond section. Stitch together, securing the lining and the streamers. (Make any adjustments necessary on the diagonal section so it matches the diamond section.) Join the 7½" ends of the 7½" x 40½" white piece. Slide inside the diamond section. Stitch on the stitching line of the top edge of the diamond section. Unfold diagonal section and lining.

5. **Attach folded triangles.** Fold all A pieces into quarters; press. Pin the raw edges to the top edge of the windsock. Add the remaining folded triangles, sliding the second one between the folded edges of the previous triangle. Adjust the triangles to fit. Baste to the top edge of the windsock, securing the lining in the stitching.

6. **Complete windsock.** Fold the white bias strips to measure 1½" wide. Stitch to the top of the windsock with raw edges matching. Fold over the macrame hoop and slipstitch to the inside of the windsock. Mark four equal intervals on the bias. Cut two 1-yard pieces of cording. Secure to the inside edge of the windsock, attaching the ends of the same piece opposite each other. Knot together in the center to make a loop. ❖

Schematic

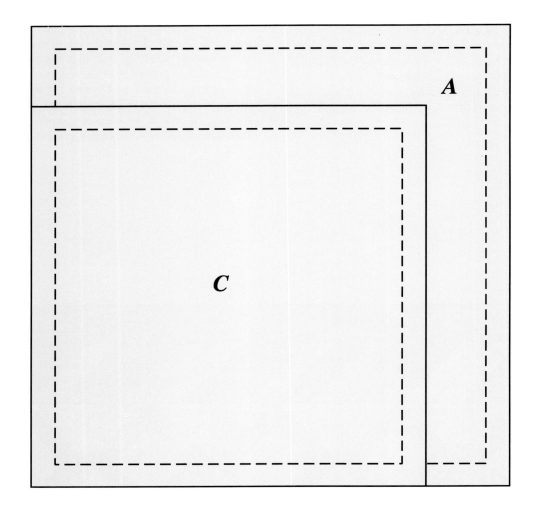

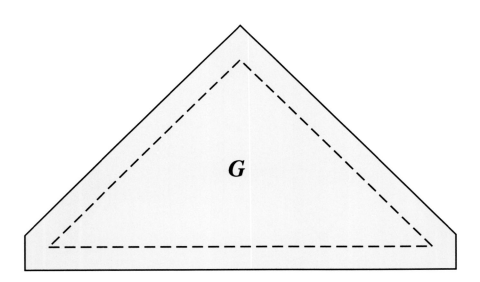

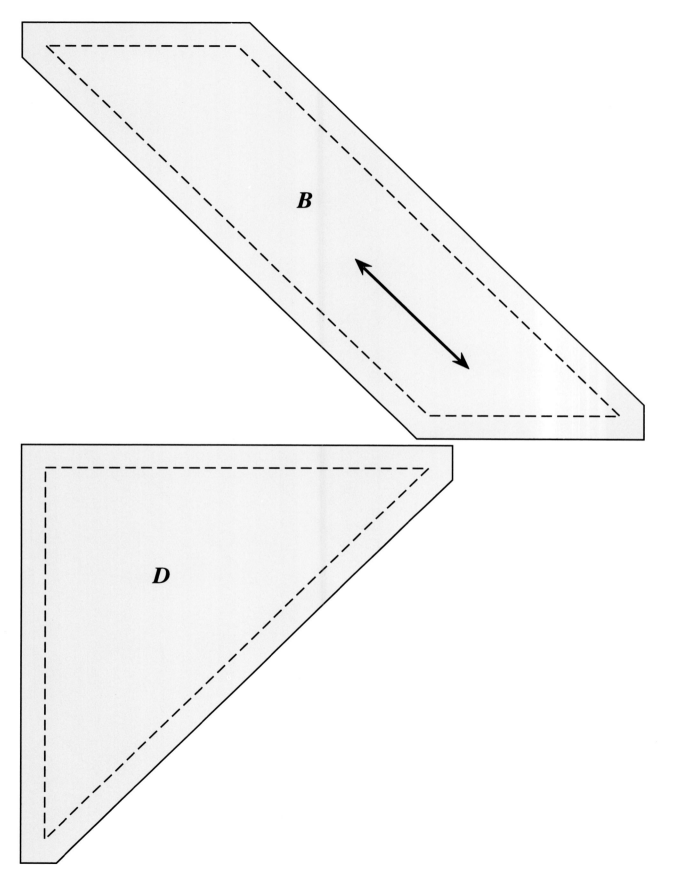

B

D

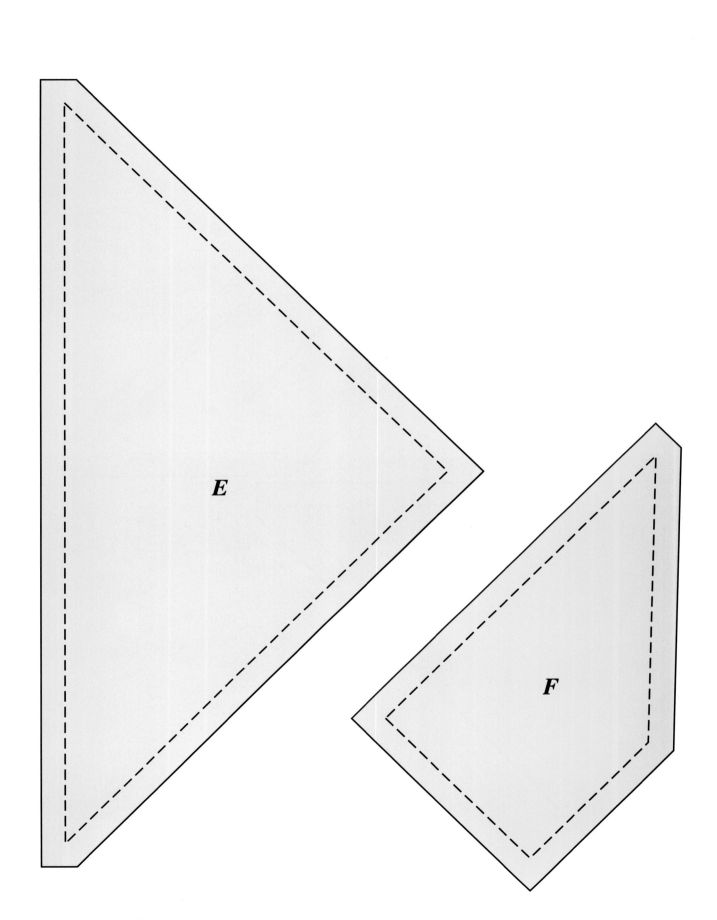

E

F

Funny Bunnies

Those who are forever young at heart will hop for joy when they spy these cute little bunnies just made for fun. Pieced from an old quilt, they're a precious way to bring an old heirloom to life.

Materials (for one bunny):

Scrap from an old quilt:
   One BODY for front

Scrap of pink fabric:
   One BODY for back
   Four EARs
   One FACE

½ yard of ⅜"-wide white satin
   ribbon
One purchased ½"-wide pink
   ribbon rose with stem
Stuffing
Acrylic paints:
   lavender and burgundy
Fine paint brush
Green embroidery floss
Thread for construction

Directions:

1. **Construct ears.** Join two EARs, leaving an opening. Clip the curves. Turn. Topstitch through all of the layers as indicated (see pattern). Paint the inside of the ear (see photo). Allow the paint to dry. Repeat for the second ear. Make a tuck in the base of each ear; baste.

2. **Construct body.** Pin the base of the ears to the right side of the head on the BODY front. Stitch the BODY front to the BODY back, leaving an opening and being sure to secure the ears in the seam. Machine stitch a vertical line in the bottom of the bunny to form the legs (see pattern). Clip the curves. Turn. Stuff the bunny firmly. Slipstitch the opening closed.

3. **Complete bunny.** Cross-stitch the eyes on the FACE using green floss. Paint the nose, mouth and whiskers (Diagram 1).

Diagram 1

Allow to dry. Fold the raw edges of the FACE under ¼". Center and slipstitch the FACE to the bunny head front (quilted side). Fold the tips of the bunny's ears ¾" to the front; tack.

Tie a 12" piece of ribbon around the bunny's neck in a bow. Wrap the stem of the ribbon rose around the knot in the center of the bow (see photo). ❖

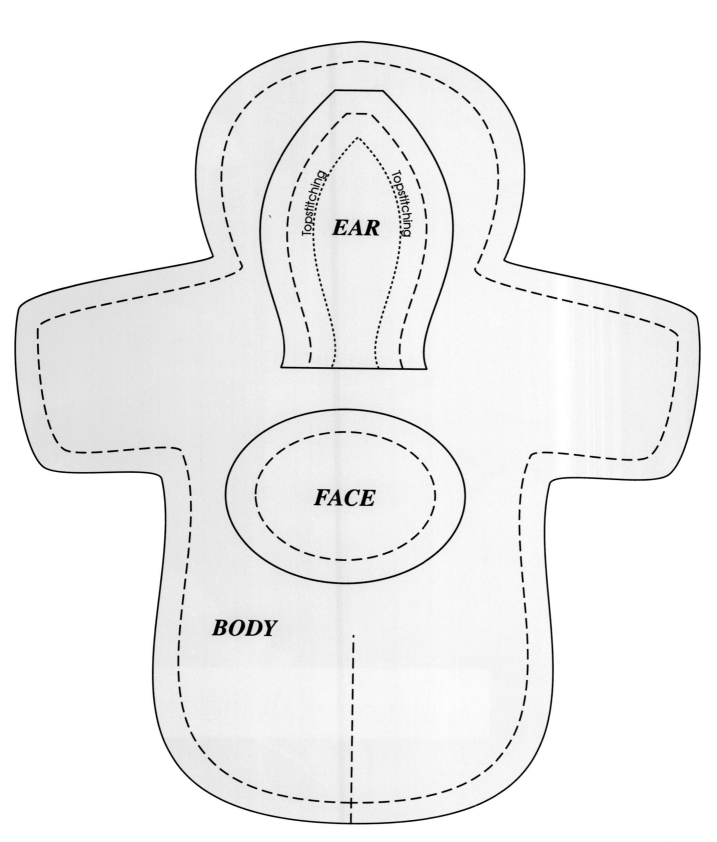

EAR

Topstitching

Topstitching

FACE

BODY

Cathedral Window Screen

Finished size: Center panel - 16½" x 45"
  Side panels - 6½" x 38½"

Materials:

2 yards of light-green-print fabric:
  Two of Template A
  One 14" x 16" piece*
  Two 6½" x 7½" pieces*
  Two 7" x 40" backing pieces*
  One 18" x 48" backing piece*

1 yard of green-print fabric:
  Two 2¼" x 31" strips*
  One 2¼" x 16" strip*
  7½ yards of 2"-wide bias

½ yard of scraps of four to six
different print and solid fabrics:
  One of Template F
  Two of Template H
  10"-long strips cut into widths
  varying from ½" to 1"

¼ yard blue fabric:
  12 of Template C

¼ yard of purple-print fabric:
  Two 6½" x 12" pieces*

⅛ yard of purple-stripe fabric:
  Four 1" x 20½" strips*

Scrap of pink-print fabric:
  Two of Template G
  Two of Template D

Scrap of lavender fabric:
  One of Template B

Scrap of blue-print fabric:
  12 of Template B

Scrap of sage-print fabric:
  Eight of Template E

1½ yards of fleece:
  One 18" x 48" piece*
  Two 7" x 40" pieces*

Green, pink, and dark-pink
  fabric paints
Manila folder for stencilling
Craft knife
Stencil brush
Small brush
Dark-green embroidery floss
Thread for construction
Matching thread for quilting
Seven assorted green buttons
Screen frame

*These pieces can be adjusted
as needed to fit the screen.

Strip-piecing reaches new heights in this creative screen that captures the serene effect of a stained glass cathedral window. It's sure to be a conversation piece in any room.

Directions:

1. **Make painted blocks.** Trace Template C onto
   the blue fabric 12 times. Mark the center of the
   blocks. Transfer the two stencil patterns to the
   manila folder. Cut out pattern with a craft
   knife. Center and stencil the pink leaves and
   diamond, then the green flowers. With a small
   brush, add dark-pink paint to the two edges of
   the center pink diamond (Diagram 1). Cut out
   Cs when the paint is dry.

   Using dark-green floss, outline stitch around
   each green flower. Buttonhole and outline
   stitch as desired on the upper section of the
   center panel (see photo and Diagram 7).

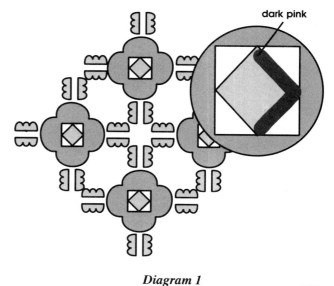

dark pink

Diagram 1

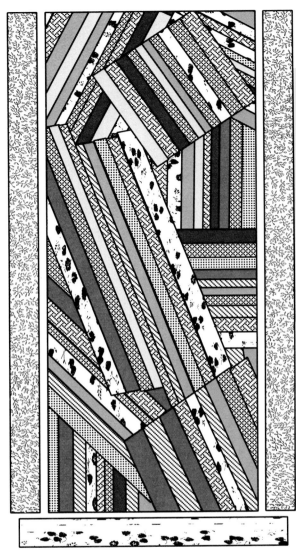

Diagram 2

2. **Make center panel.** For the lower section, strip-piece 10" lengths (from ½" to 1" wide) of fabrics in different combinations to make three 10" x 14" pieces. (Using the wrong side of the same fabrics produces a unique effect.) Cut the pieces into sections as desired and piece together to make a 12½" x 31" piece. Stitch one 2¼" x 31" green-print strip to each side of the pieced panel. Stitch one 2¼" x 16" green-print strip to the bottom of the pieced panel (Diagram 2).

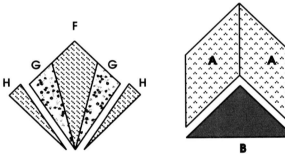

Diagram 3   *Diagram 4*

To make one pieced C , join the two pink-print Gs to the long edges of the F. Join the two Hs to the long edges of the pieced G/F/G section (Diagram 3).

Join the long edges of the two light-green-print As, then set in the lavender B (Diagram 4). Join the pieced C, four painted Cs and two pink-print Ds (Diagram 5). Set in the A/A/B piece, stitching to, but not through the seam allowances of the C and D pieces. Applique the pieced upper part to the 14" x 16" light-green-print piece, centering the pieced section on the bottom edge. Join the upper and lower sections of the center panel.

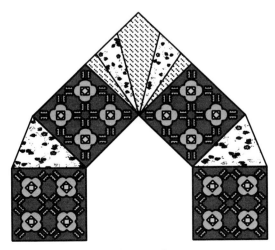

Diagram 5

Diagram 6

3. **Make side panel.** Using four painted Cs, six blue-print Bs and four sage-print Es, piece the center section in diagonal rows (Diagram 6). Join the rows together. Join one 1" x 20½" purple-strip piece to each side of the pieced panel. Join a 6½" x 7½" light-green-print piece to the top of the pieced panel and a 6½" x 12" purple-print piece to the bottom of the pieced panel. Repeat to make the second panel.

4. **Quilt panels.** Mark the embroidery and quilting lines in the upper center section (Diagram 7). Mark the quilting lines in all of the painted blocks in the side panels the same as the upper center section (Diagram 7). Then mark channel quilting lines 1" apart on the side panels from the top to the bottom of the pieced section, outside the painted blocks (Diagram 8). Layer the light-green-print fabric, fleece, and the design panel piece. Baste. Repeat for the two remaining pieces. Quilt on all of the marked lines and the seam lines using green thread. In the lower section of the center panel, quilt some of the seam lines as desired. In the lower section of the side panels, quilt at random, following the pattern in the print fabric. Sew the buttons onto the upper section of the center panel.

5. **Complete panels.** Recheck all of the measurements, aligning the seams which join the upper sections of each panel and allowing for casings at the top and the bottom of each of the panels. Bind the sides of the panels with the green-print bias. Fold the top and the bottom edges double to the back side to make the casings. Install in the frame. ❖

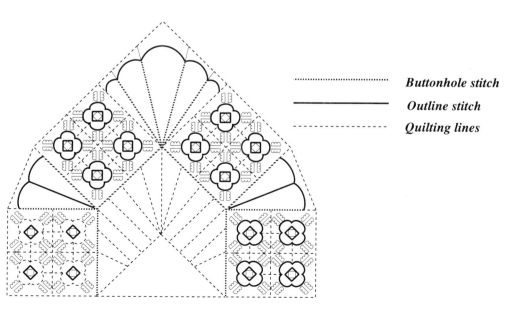

Diagram 7

··························· **Buttonhole stitch**

———————————— **Outline stitch**

– – – – – – – – – – **Quilting lines**

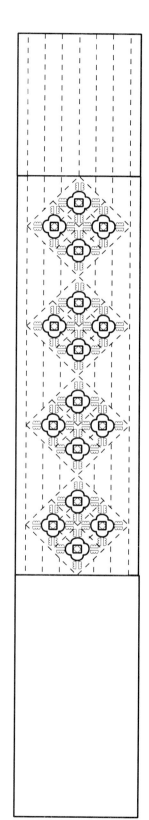

Diagram 8

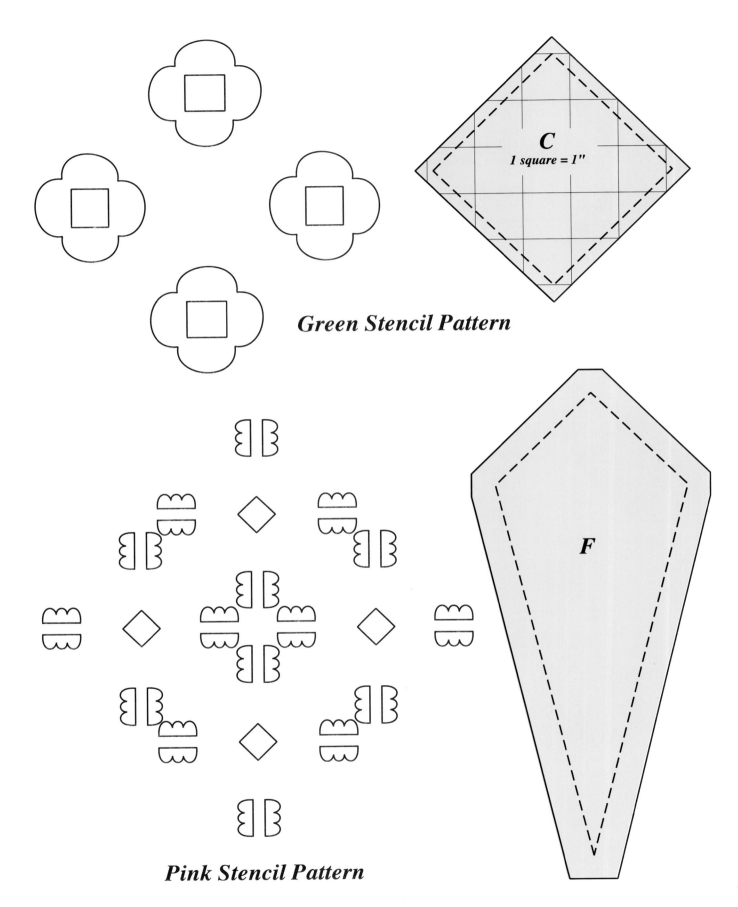

Green Stencil Pattern

C
1 square = 1"

F

Pink Stencil Pattern

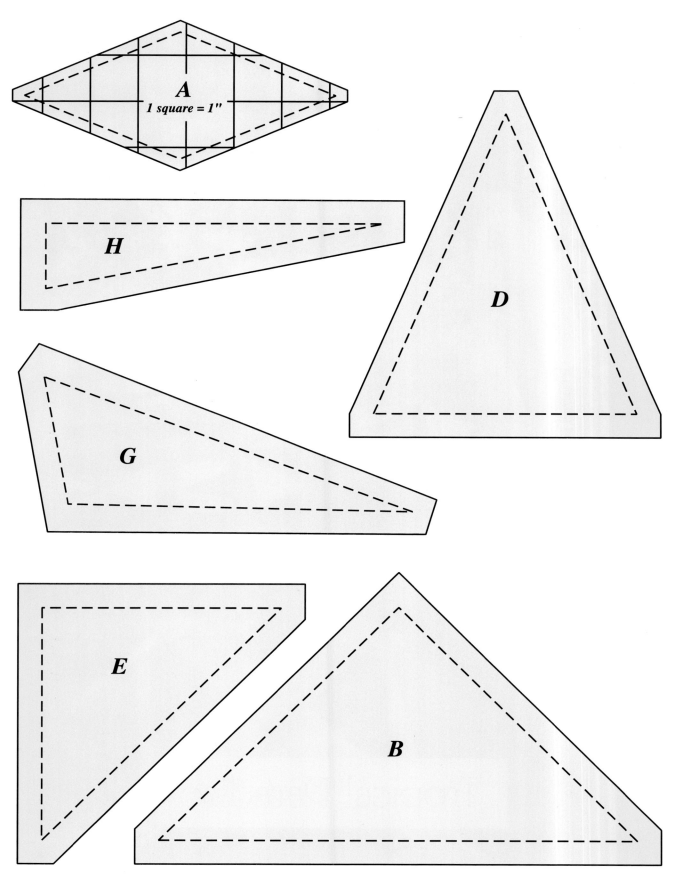

A
1 square = 1"

H

D

G

E

B

Tropical Paradise

Directions:

1. **Prepare strips.** Join the 44"-long strips on the long edges in the following order:

   Two sets of 1½" green and 2" blue
   Three sets of 2" turquoise and 1½" green
   One set of 1½" turquoise and 2" blue
   One set of 1½" blue and 2" turquoise
   One set of 1½" blue and 2" green

   Cut two mirror image Ds from each set of the strips (Diagram 1). Note that the dotted line on Template D is the seam line of the strips.

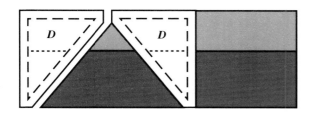

Diagram 1

2. **Piece fish design.** To make four yellow side sections, join two pieced Ds to one yellow A (Diagram 2) in the following color sequences:

Back fish:	green/blue, turquoise/ green
Top fish:	green/turquoise, blue/green
Center fish:	turquoise/blue, turquoise/green
Bottom fish:	blue/turquoise, green/blue

   To make four gold side sections, repeat in a mirror image, joing D pieces to gold As (Diagram 3).

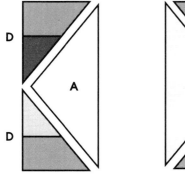 

Diagram 2   *Diagram 3*

Quilt a sample of paradise lost as it might be found under the deep blue sea—a must for your poolside gatherings.

Finished size: 7" x 22" (back)
16" x 21" (seat)

Materials:

⅛ yard of yellow fabric:
   Four of Template A
   16 of Template C
   Eight 2½" x 1½" pieces

⅛ yard of gold fabric:
   Four of Template A

Scrap of purple fabric:
   Four of Template B

⅛ yard of magenta fabric:
   Four 1½" x 5½" strips

⅛ yard of pink-stripe fabric:
   Four 1½" x 5½" strips

¼ yard of blue fabric:
   Three of Template C
   Two 2½" x 1½" strips
   Five 2" x 44" strips
   Two 1½" x 44" strips

2 yards of turquoise fabric:
   Four of Template C
   One 2½" x 1½" piece
   Five 2" x 44" strips
   One 1½" x 44" strip
   One piece like back (see Step 3)
   One piece like seat (see Step 3)

¼ yard of green fabric:
   One of Template C
   Five 2½" x 1½" pieces
   Two 2" x 44" strips
   Five 1½" x 44" strips

Purchased director's chair (see photo)
Yellow paint

To make one center section, join
two yellow Cs to one purple B.
Then add two yellow 2½" x 1½"
pieces to yellow Cs (Diagram 4).
Join one magenta piece and one
pink-stripe piece to the long edges
of the pieced section (Diagram 5).
Repeat to make four center sections.

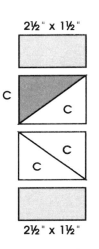

Diagram 4

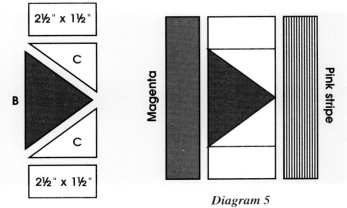

Diagram 5

To make four tail sections, join the long edges of two Cs in the
following color sequences:

Three sets of yellow/blue
Four sets of yellow/turquoise
One set of yellow/green

Add 2½" x 1½" strips (Diagram 6) in the following color sequences:

	Back fish	Top fish
2½" x 1½" strip	green	green
C/C pieces	yellow/blue	yellow/turquoise
C/C pieces	yellow/turquoise	yellow/blue
2½" x 1½" strip	green	green

	Center fish	Bottom fish
2½" x 1½" strip	turquoise	blue
C/C pieces	yellow/blue	yellow/turquoise
C/C pieces	yellow/turquoise	yellow/green
2½" x 1½" strip	green	blue

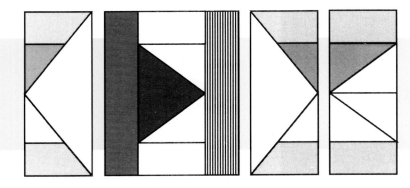

Diagram 6

Join the four sections to make
one fish (Diagram 7). Repeat to
make four fishes.

Diagram 7

3. **Complete chair.** Remove the canvas panels from the purchased director's chair, familiarizing yourself with how the panels are attached.

Our model has casings on each short end of the back panel and the seat. The back panel's casings slide over the wooden slats and into the channels on each side of the seat. To get to these channels, the hinged chair sides must be hanging down. The channels or the chair may be one of two styles: on the outside with a seat panel which wraps all the way over the chair edges, or on the inside with a seat panel which wraps just part of the way over the edges. For both types, construction is the same. Remove the stitching of the casings from the original canvas panels. Measure the panels.

Join eight strip sets on the long edges in the color sequences identified in Step 2 to make four new strip sets.

To make the back panel, cut the back fish strip set into two equal lengths. Stitch one strip set to each end of the back fish, matching the strip's colors (see Back Seat Schematic). Then stitch one 2" x 44" turquoise strip across the top and one 2" x 44" blue strip across the bottom of the back. Trim excess fabric. Match the center of the design (point on purple B) to the center of the canvas back panel. Trim the design piece to ½" longer on all edges than the canvas back panel. Cut one piece from the turquoise fabric for backing the same size as the design piece. With right sides together, stitch the back and design piece on the long edges,

leaving an opening. Turn. Insert the canvas back panel. Ensure the design piece is slightly looser than the canvas panel so all of the stress is on the panel. Slipstitch the opening closed. Fold the casings to the back on the short ends. Topstitch securely.

To make the seat, cut one each of the following lengths from the remaining strip sets (these lengths are going to be joined to each side of the fish design— the left side measurement is given first, then the right):

Top fish: 9", 11"
Center fish: 6", 14"
Bottom fish: 14", 5"

Stitch the strip sets to the ends of the fish designs, matching the colors. Place the fish designs together, aligning the center seams (see Seat Schematic); stitch. Then stitch one 2" x 44" green strip to the top of the design section and one 2" x 44" blue strip to the bottom of the section. Match the center of the design to the center of the canvas seat panel. Trim the design piece to ½" larger on all edges than the canvas seat panel. Cut one piece from the turquoise fabric the same size as the design piece for backing. With the right sides together, stitch the design piece and the backing, leaving an opening. Turn. Insert the canvas seat panel, again ensuring that the design piece is slightly looser than the canvas panel. Finish like the back panel.

Paint the chair; allow it to dry. Then attach all of the panels. ❖

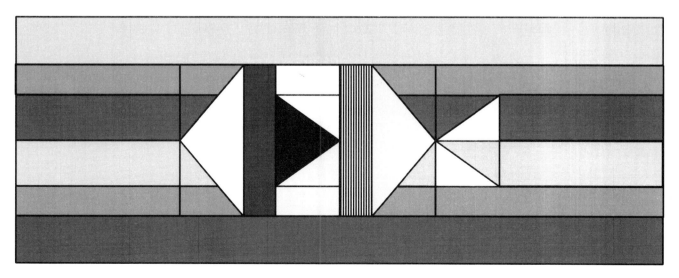

Back Seat Schematic

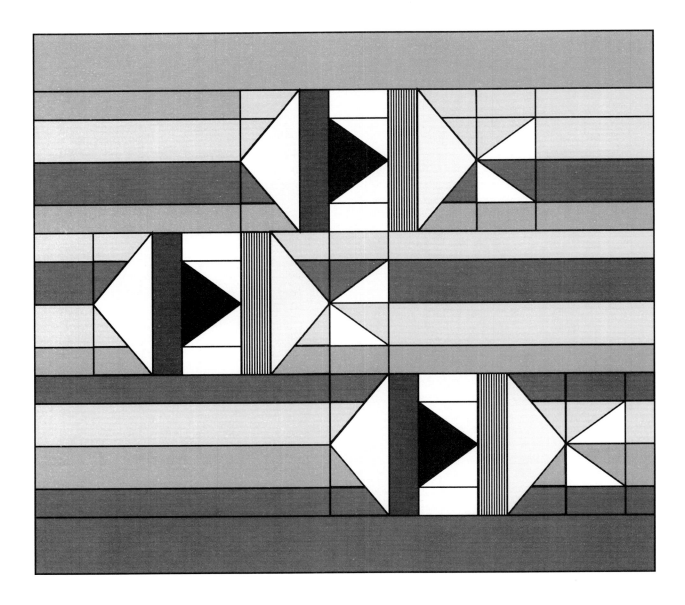

Seat Schematic

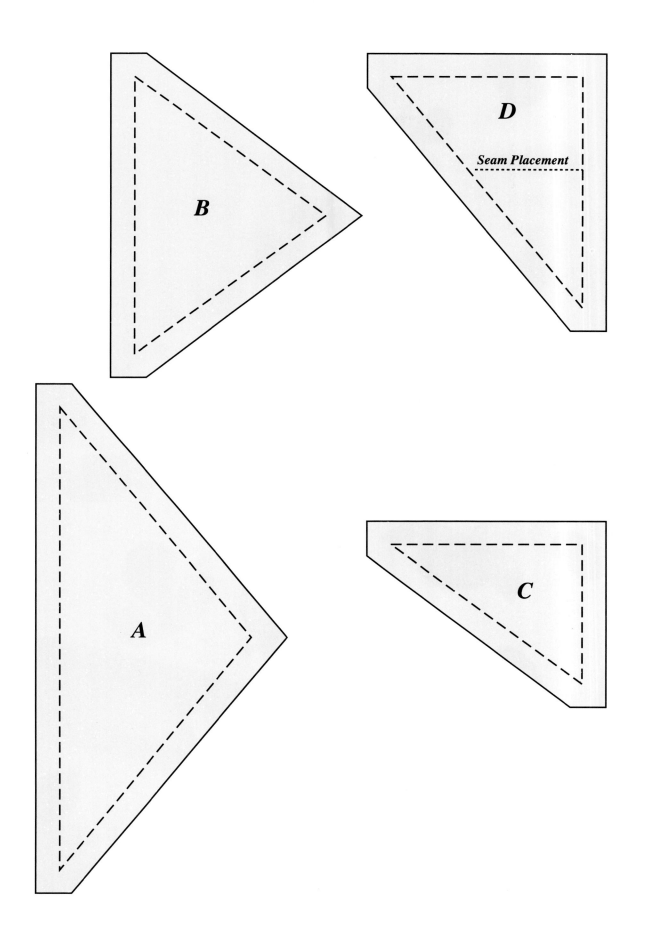

B

D

Seam Placement

A

C

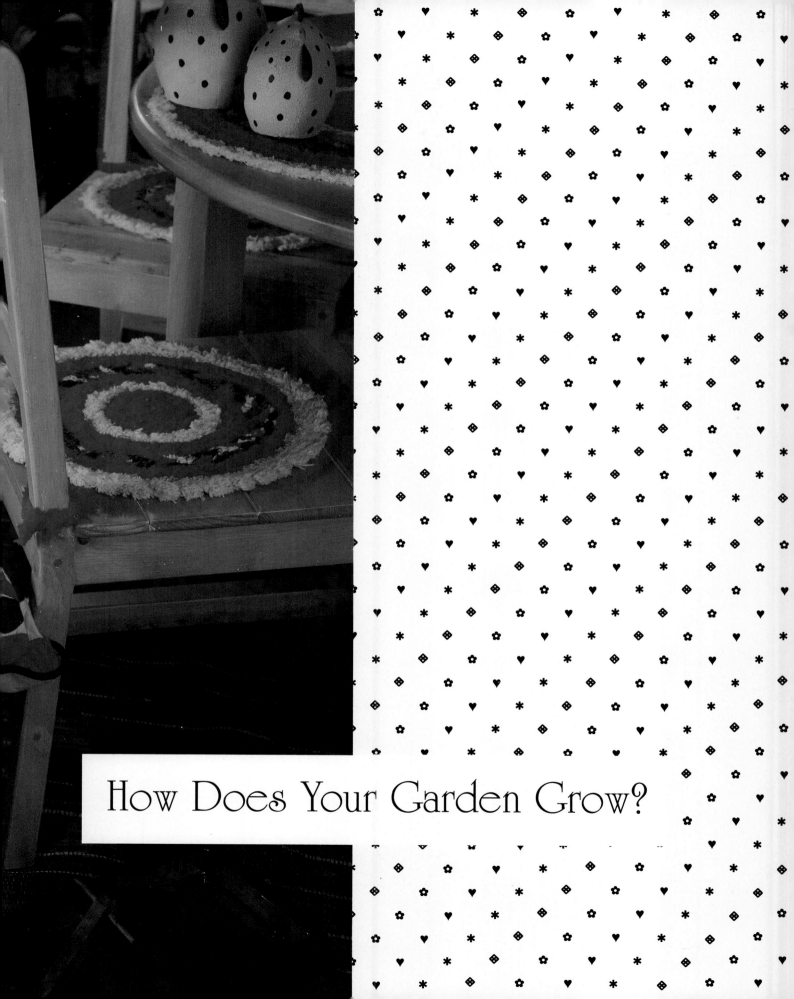

How Does Your Garden Grow?

Fruity Floor Pillows

Feast your eyes on these delectable overstuffed floor pillows. Cozy enough for two, you'll delight in their sumptuous comfort.

Finished size: 35" X 35"

Materials:

6 yards of muslin:
Two 37" x 37" pieces
Two 35" x 35" pieces
Four 16½" x 16½" pieces

1 yard of red fabric:
Four 2" x 36" border strips
Four APPLEs
16 PEARs

1 yard of green fabric:
40 LEAFs
20 STEMs
20 of Template A
4 yards of 2"-wide bias
for corded piping

1 yard of polyester fleece:
One 35" x 35" piece

Seven pounds of stuffing
Thread for construction
Cream thread for quilting

Directions:

1. **Make pillow top.** Mark an "X" from corner-to-corner on the four 16½" x 16½" muslin pieces. Then draw a line from the top to the bottom through the center of each block. Join two of the pieces. Repeat to make two sets. Then join the sets on the long edges (Diagram 1).

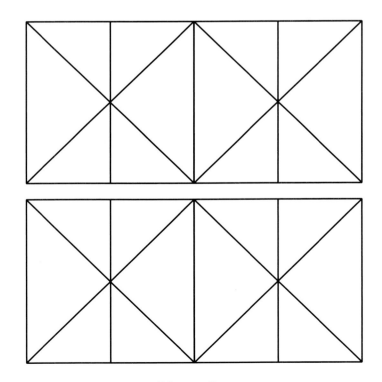

Diagram 1

Place one pear on a diagonal line with the top 1¾" from corner. Slide one green A under the notch at the bottom. Applique notch, then all of the pear. Repeat, placing one pear in each corner of all four muslin pieces. Place one apple in the center of one muslin piece with the notch on the vertical line. Slide a green A under the notch at the bottom. Applique the notch, then all of the apple. Repeat in the center of each muslin piece, placing the apples in the same direction or in opposite pairs, as desired. Applique the stem to the center top of each pear and apple, then applique the leaves (see schematic).

2. **Add border.** Center and stitch one red strip to each edge of the pillow top. Miter the corners.

3. **Complete top.** Mark all quilting lines (see schematic), working from the center out. Layer one 35" x 35" muslin piece, batting, and the pillow top. Baste. Quilt on all of the marked lines and around the outside edge of each appliqued motif.

4. **Finish pillow.** Make four yards of corded piping. Stitch the cording to the outside edge of the red border. With the right sides together, stitch the second 35" x 35" muslin piece to the pillow top, sewing on the stitching line of the cording and leaving one edge open.

For the pillow form, stitch two 37" x 37" pieces of muslin together, leaving an opening on one edge. Turn. Stuff moderately. Slipstitch the opening closed. Insert the pillow form; slipstitch the opening closed. ❖

Schematic

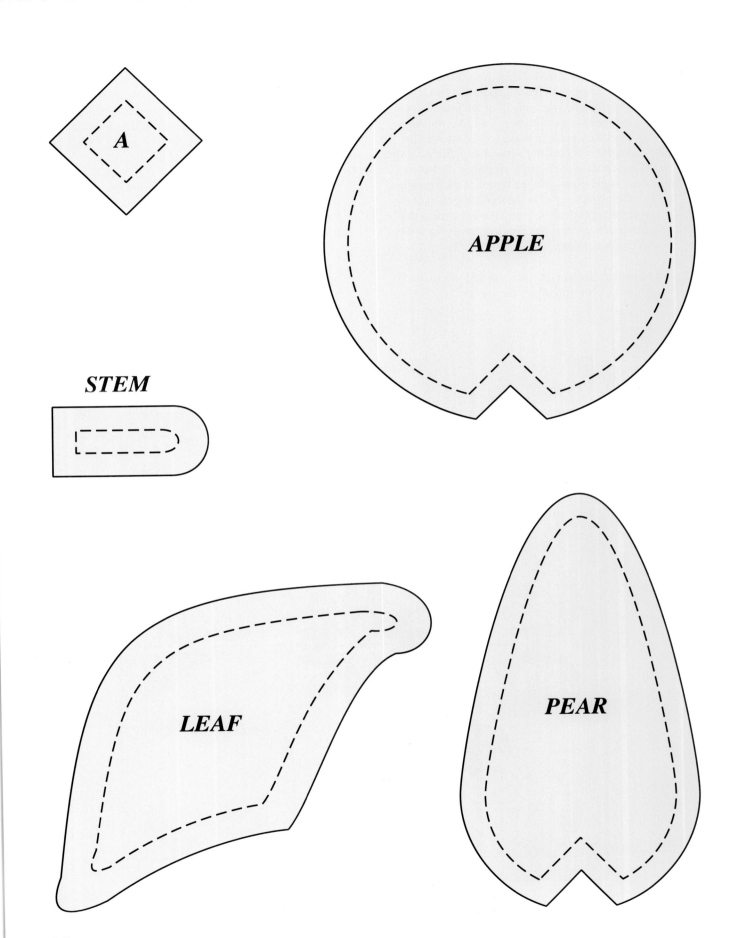

A

APPLE

STEM

LEAF

PEAR

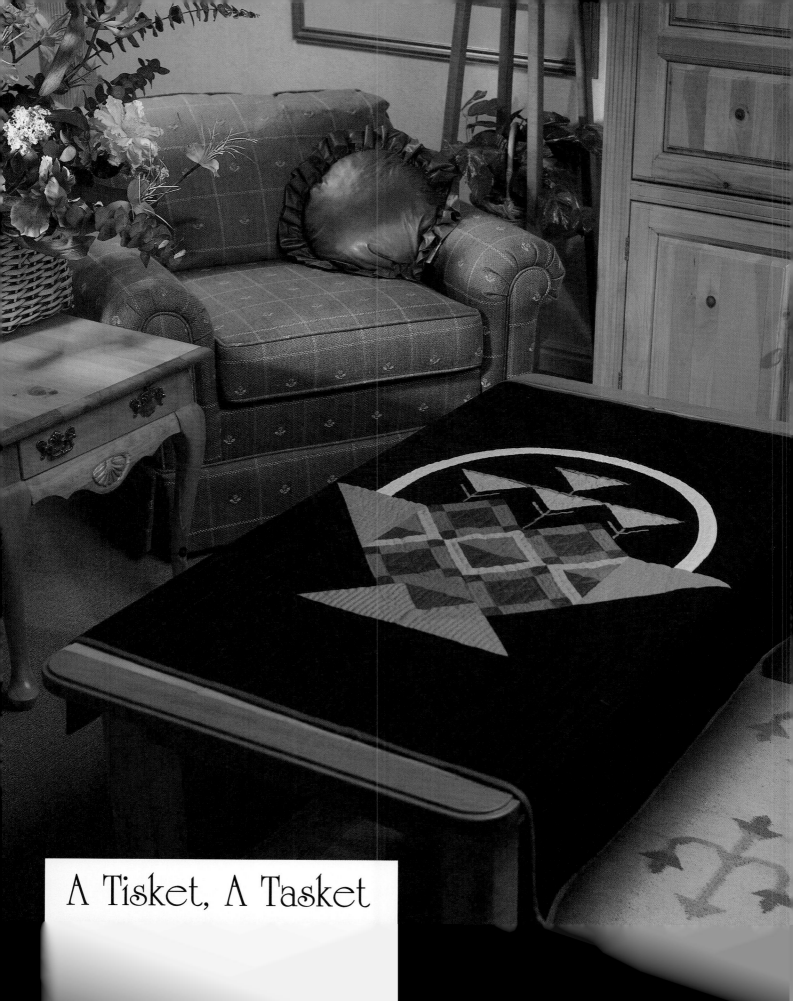

A Tisket, A Tasket

This oversized basket in hues of blue promises to cheer you through every season.

Finished size: 41" x 47"

Materials:

2⅜ yards of black fabric:
    One 41" x 47" front piece
    One 43" x 49" backing piece

1 yard of red fabric:
    Two of Template B
    Two 1½" x 12" strips
    One 3½" x 14" strip
    One 2¼" x 22" strip
    5 yards of 1½"-wide bias for binding

¼ yard of green fabric:
    Two of Template B
    Two 1½" x 14" strips
    One 3½" x 12" strip
    One 2½" x 22" strip

¼ yard of turquoise fabric:
    Two 1½" x 22" strips
    Four of Template F

⅛ yard of blue fabric:
    Two of Template C
    Two of Template D
    Two of Template E

½ yard of cream fabreic:
    One HANDLE

1⅜ yards of polyester fleece:
    One 43" x 49" piece

Thread for construction
Blue thread for quilting
Turquoise paint
Manila folder for stencilling template
Craft knife
Stencil brush

Directions:

1. **Make four-corner blocks.** Join two 1½" x 12" red strips to one 3½" x 12" green strip on the long edges. Cut these into 1½"-wide segments. Then join two 1½" x 14" green strips to one 3½" x 14" red strip on the long edges. Cut these into 3½"-wide segments. Join two red/green/red sets to one green/red/green set (Diagram 1) to make one four-corner block. Repeat to make four four-corner blocks.

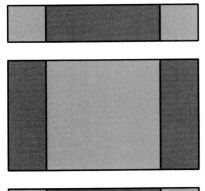

Diagram 1

2. **Make triangle blocks.** Join one 1½" x 22" turquoise strip to one 2¼" x 22" red strip on the long edges. Then join one 1½" x 22" turquoise strip to one 2½" x 22" green strip on the long edges. Cut four of Template A from each set, noting placement of the seam.

Join two turquoise/green As on the short edges, matching the seams. Join two turquoise/red As. Then join the sets to complete one center block (Diagram 2). Join one turquoise/green A to one turquoise/red A on the short edges. Repeat to make one mirror-image set.

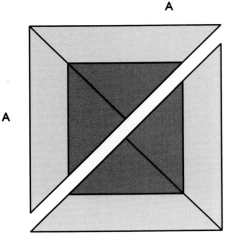

A

A

Diagram 2

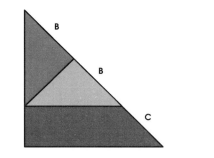

Diagram 3

To make center bottom block, join one green B to one red B on the short edges. Repeat to make one mirror-image set. Join one blue C to each B/B set (Diagram 3). Join B/B/C sets on long edges.

3. **Piece basket.** Join blocks in rows, using blue Ds and Es (Diagram 4). Join rows to complete basket.

4. **Complete quilt top.** Mark placement for the HANDLE, FLOWERs (turquoise Fs) and BASKET on the 41" x 47" front piece (see schematic). Applique the HANDLE, then the BASKET and FLOWERs. Transfer the stencil pattern for the STEM to the manila folder. Cut out pattern with a craft knife. Stencil stems below each flower, noting that top flower has no branches and that the right and left flowers have shorter stems. Then paint a ½"-wide band across the top edge of each flower, using the straight edge of the folder to make the top edge even.

5. **Complete quilt.** Mark quilting lines (Diagram 6). Layer the quilt backing, fleece and quilt top. Baste. Quilt all marked lines with blue thread. Also quilt around each appliqued piece. Bind with red bias. Miter the corners. ❖

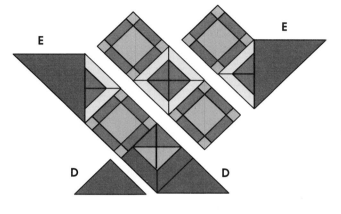

Diagram 4

Schematic

Diagram 5

HANDLE

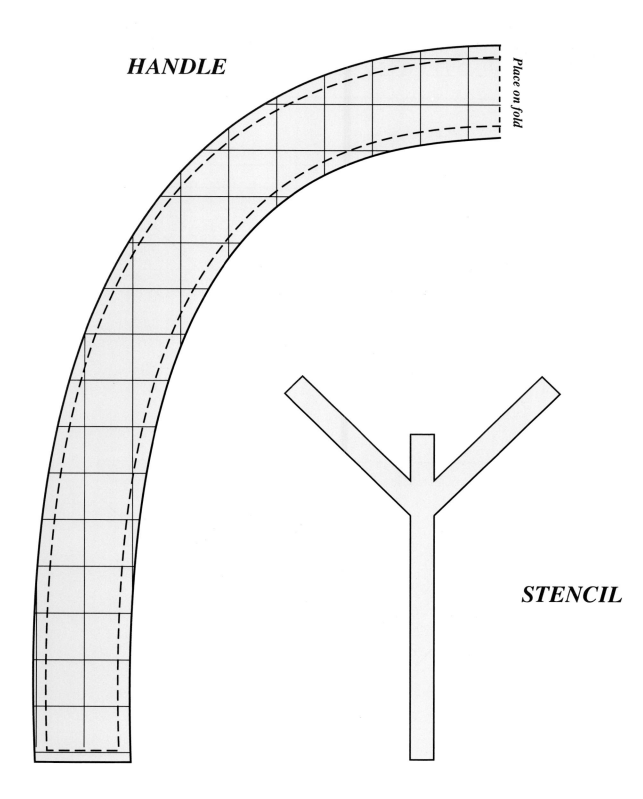

Place on fold

STENCIL

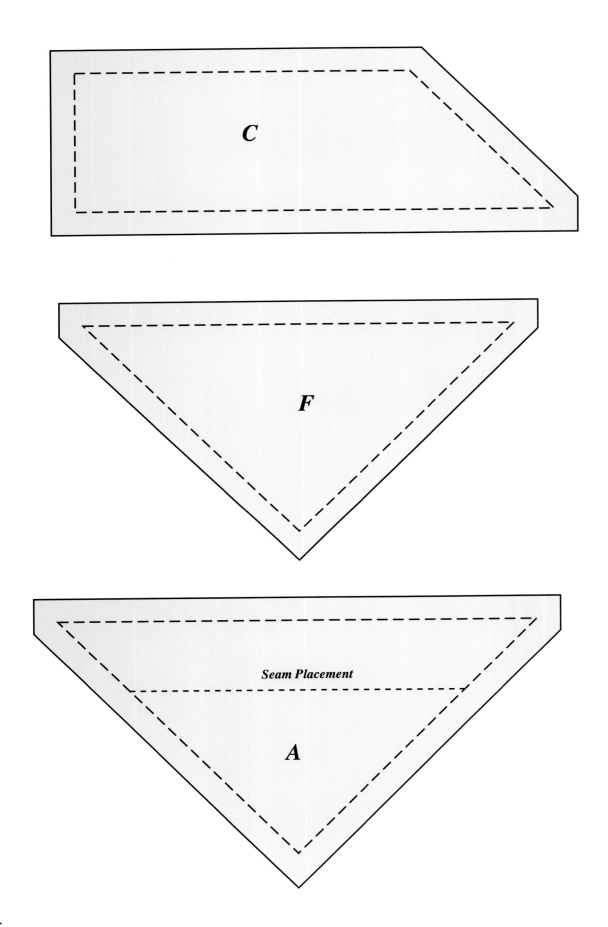

C

F

Seam Placement

A

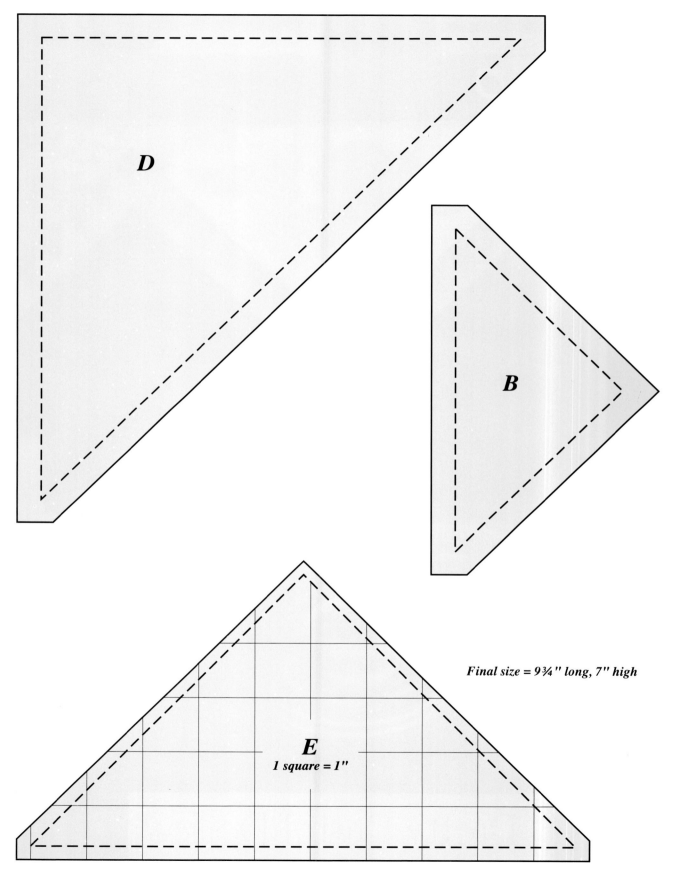

D

B

E

1 square = 1"

Final size = 9¾" long, 7" high

Pretty Pastel Doilies

Directions:

1. **Prepare fabrics for painted center doily** (see photo). Cut the following fabrics:
   One 14" x 14" piece of light-weight canvas
   14 of Template A from burgundy print
   14 of Template A from lavender print
   One Template B from lavender
   Two 1¾" x 6" pieces from lavender
   One 1½" x 17" piece from lavender
   One 16" x 16" x 23" piece from muslin
      for backing
   1¾ yards of 1"-wide tan bias tape

2. **Make triangle.** Fold the canvas piece to make a triangle; cut on the fold (Diagram 1).

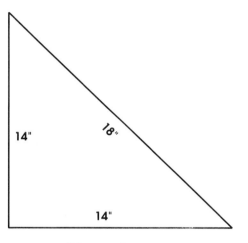

Diagram 1

3. **Paint design.** Enlarge the Flower Painting Pattern 175%. Trace the design onto the canvas. Paint the design using the colors listed in the materials (see photo). Center and trim the canvas, making the short edges 13" and the long edge 18".

4. **Add borders.** Join the 1½" x 17" lavender piece to the top edge of the design piece. Join the long edges of one burgundy-print A and one lavender A (Diagram 2). Repeat to make 14 sets.

Diagram 2

Line your shelves, adorn your mantle, or accent your favorite family heirloom with these quaintly quilted doilies.

Finished Size: 15½" x 15½" x 22"

Materials:

½ yard of light-weight canvas

¼ yard of burgundy-print fabric

Scraps of:
   large-print fabric
   mauve-print fabric
   light-green-print fabric
   cream fabric
   lavender fabric
   pink fabric
   grey fabric
   tan fabric
   mulberry fabric

1 yard of muslin

5 yards of 1"-wide tan bias tape
Thread for construction
Gold thread for quilting
Acrylic paints:
   lemon yellow, yellow,
   pink, rose, lavender,
   light green, green
   light blue, blue

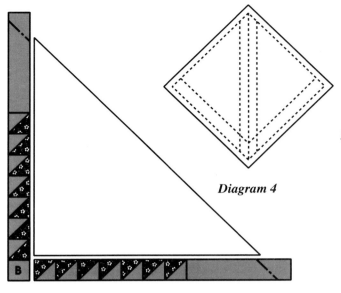

Diagram 4

Diagram 3

Join the sets to make two rows of seven A/A sets. Place both rows so the burgundy-print As are next to the design piece. Stitch one 1¾" x 6" piece to the end of one row. Stitch the lavender B and the second 1¾" x 6" piece to the ends of the second row of A/As (Diagram 3). Attach the short row, then the long row to the design piece.

5. **Complete center doily.** Layer the muslin and the design piece. Baste. Quilt with gold thread around each part of the painted design. Then echo quilt to fill the whole design piece. Quilt ¹⁄₁₆" from the seam of the lavender As and B. Quilt the lavender B (Diagram 4). Trim the muslin back to match the design piece. Bind the short edges, then the long edge with the tan bias tape.

Painted Center Doily Schematic

6. **Prepare fabrics for pink doily.** Cut the following fabrics:
   One of Template C from grey
   One 4½" x 4½" piece from cream
   Two of Template D from large print
   One of Template E from large print
   16 of Template A from burgundy print
   16 of Template A from pink

One of Template B from pink
Two 1¾" x 6" pieces from pink
One ¾" x 8½" strip from mauve print
One 1" x 7" strip from mauve print
Two 1" x 8½" strips from light-green print
One 1½" x 17½" piece from tan
One 16" x 16" x 23" piece from muslin for backing
1¾ yards of tan bias tape

7. Make design piece for pink doily. Applique the grey C to the center of the cream 4½" x 4½" piece. Trace the Stencil Pattern on the C; paint (see photo).

Join the bottom edge of the cream piece to the long edge of the large-print E (Diagram 5). Join one 8½" green-print strip to one 8½" mauve-print strip on the long edges with the right sides together. Then join the second 8½" green-print strip to the mauve-print strip on the long edges with the wrong side of the green-print being treated as the right side. From the green/mauve/green strip, cut two mirror image Fs with the right side of the green-print on the long edge of the template (Diagram 6).

Diagram 5

Diagram 6

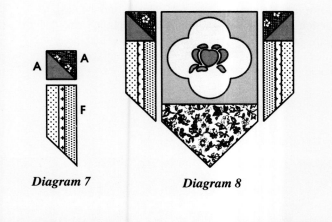

Stitch one burgundy-print A to one pink A on the long edges (Diagram 2, pg. 151). Repeat to make two sets. Join one pink edge to the top of the green/mauve/green F (Diagram 7). Repeat to make a mirror image A/A/F piece.

Diagram 7

Diagram 8

Stitch the A/A/F pieces to the sides of the cream/E piece, aligning the top edges (Diagram 8). Stitch the 7" mauve-print strip to the top edge of the design section. Then add the large-print Ds (Diagram 9).

Match the center of the 1½" x 17½" tan piece to the center top edge of the design section; stitch. Trim to the same angle as the large-print Ds (Diagram 10).

Diagram 9

Diagram 10

8. **Make triangle borders.** Repeat Step 4 of the painted center doily, using pink As and a pink B instead of from lavender.

9. **Complete pink doily.** Layer the muslin and the design section. Baste. Quilt around the painted parts. Echo quilt with gold thread ¼" inside the grey C and three rows ⅛" apart outside the gray C. Mark a diagonal line from corner-to-corner across the cream 4½" x 4½"

piece. Quilt from the corner to the outside of the echo quilting. Then quilt four parallel lines ⅛" apart on both sides of the diagonal line. Repeat for each corner of the cream piece. Also quilt next to the seam around the outside edge of the cream piece and the outside edge of the A/A/F section. Quilt ¹⁄₁₆" from the seam of each pink A. Trim the muslin back to match the design piece. Bind the short edges, then the long edge with the tan bias tape.

Pink Doily Schematic

10. Prepare fabrics for green doily. Cut the following fabrics:
One of Template C from grey
One 4½" x 4½" piece from cream
Two of Template D from blue print
One of Template E from blue print
16 of Template A from burgundy print
16 of Template A from green print
One ¾" x 8½" strip from mauve print
One 1" x 7" strip from mulberry
One 1" x 8½" strip from mulberry
One 1" x 8½" strip from pink
Two 1¾" x 6" pieces from green print
One 1½" x 17½" piece from light-green print
One 1¾" x 23" piece of light-green-print bias
One 16" x 16" x 23" piece from muslin for backing
1¼ yards of 1"-wide tan bias tape

11. Complete green doily. Complete Steps 7, 8 and 9 of the pink doily, noting the following exceptions:

A. Substitute the green-print fabric As for the pink fabric As and for the tan 1½" x 17" piece.

B. In Step 7, join one 8½" pink strip to one 8½" mauve-print strip on the long edges. Then join the 8½" mulberry strip. Cut two mirror image Template Fs from the pink/mauve/mulberry strip with the pink on the long edge of the template.

C. Bind the short edges with the tan bias tape. Bind the long edge with the green-print bias. ❖

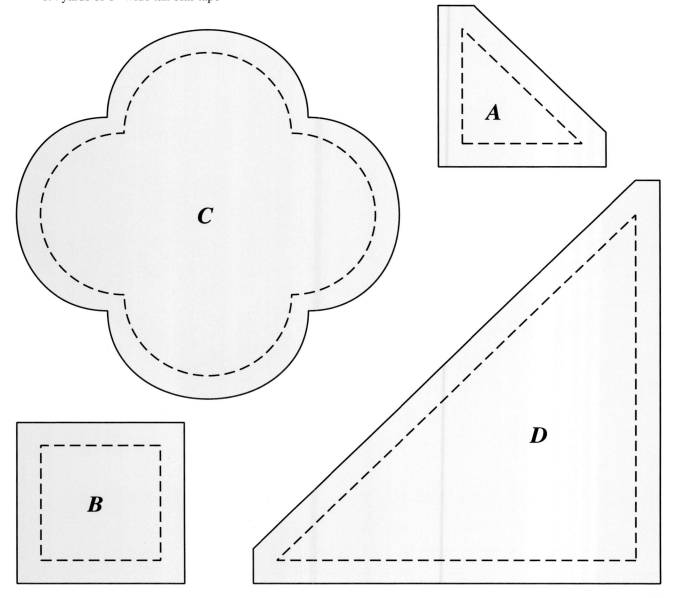

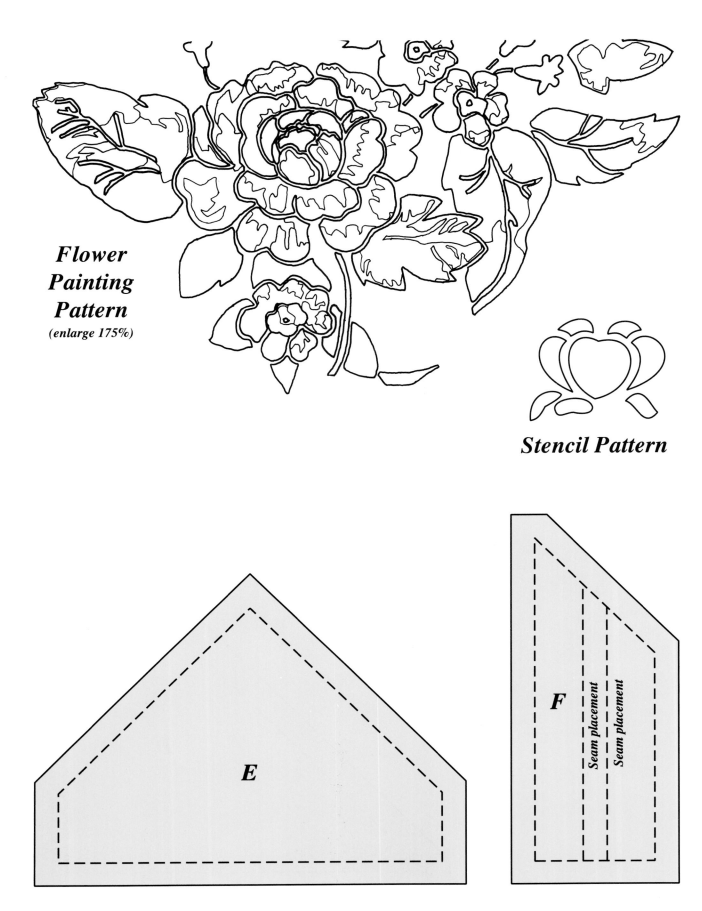

Flower Painting Pattern
(enlarge 175%)

Stencil Pattern

E

F

Seam placement

Seam placement

In the Pink

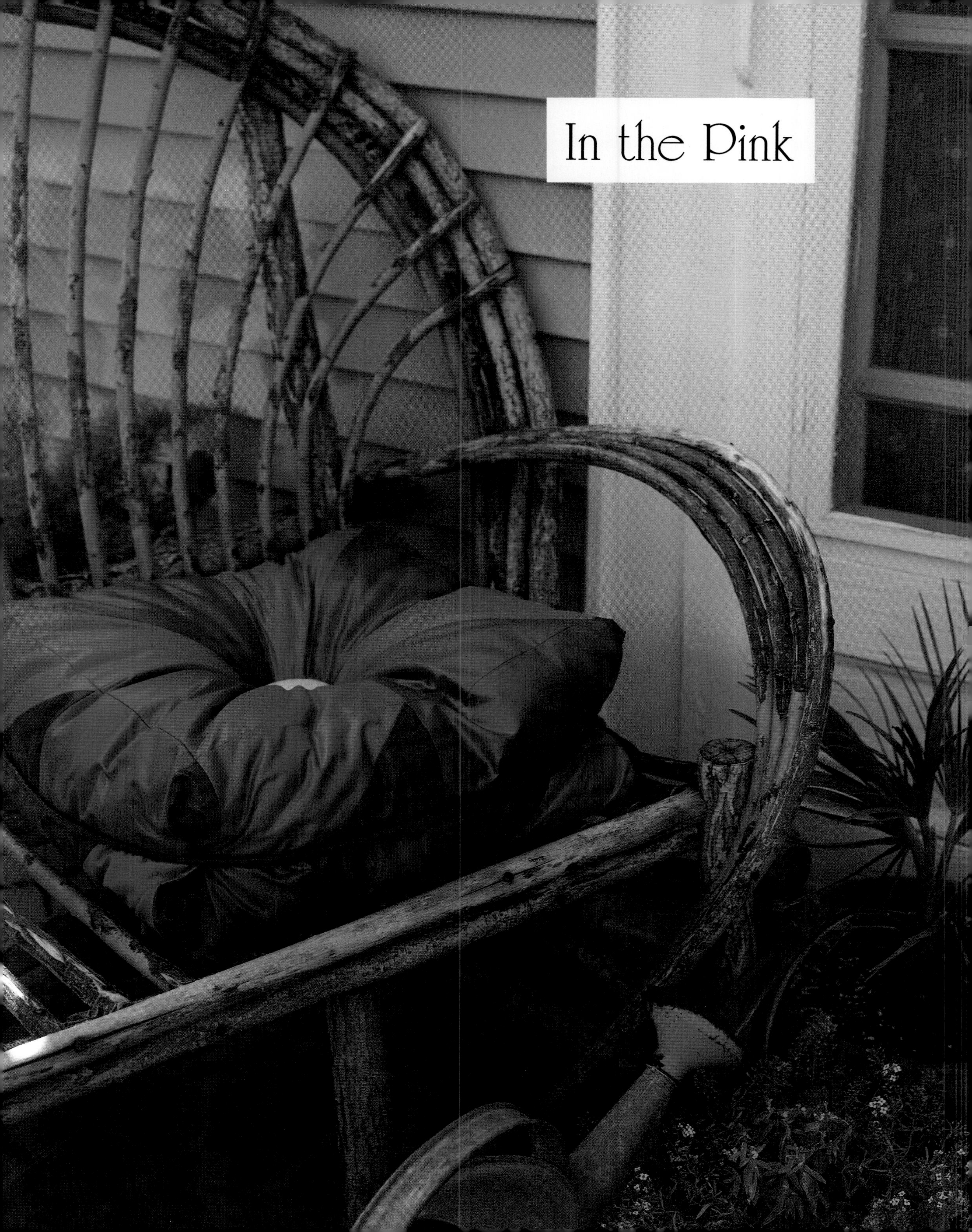

You'll feel like royalty when you cushion yourself on this fluffy, puffy pillow, fit for a queen's throne.

Finished size: 14¾" x 14¾" x 7¾"

Materials:

½ yard of purple fabric:
   Eight of Template A
   Eight of Template B

½ yard of pink fabric:
   Eight of Template A
   Eight of Template C

½ yard of dark-green fabric:
   Eight of Template D
   Eight of Template E
   61" of 2"-wide bias

1¾ yards of medium cording
Two 1¾"-wide cover buttons
Stuffing

Directions:

1. **Piece pillow top and back.** Join one purple A to one pink A (Diagram 1). Repeat to make eight A/A sets.

Diagram 1

Join one pink C to one dark-green D (Diagram 2). Repeat to make eight C/D sets.

Diagram 2

Join the sets to make rows as follows (Diagram 3):

Row 1:   dark-green E, purple B, C/D, dark-green E
Row 2:   C/D, A/A, A/A, purple B
Row 3:   purple B, A/A, A/A, C/D
Row 4:   dark-green E, C/D, purple B, dark-green E

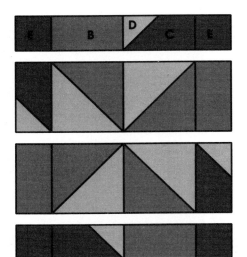

Diagram 3

Join the rows to make the pillow front. Repeat to make the pillow back.

2. **Finish pillow.** Make 1¾ yards of corded piping from the dark-green bias. Fold tucks in each corner of the front and back pieces (Diagrams 4 and 5). Baste.

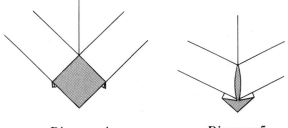

Diagram 4   *Diagram 5*

Stitch the corded piping to the right side of the pillow front, securing the tucks. Stitch the pillow front to back, sewing on the stitching line of the corded piping, securing the tucks in the pillow back and leaving an opening. Turn. Stuff the pillow. Slipstitch the opening closed.

Cover two buttons, following the manufacturer's instructions. Attach the buttons to each other through the center of the pillow. ❖

In the Pink

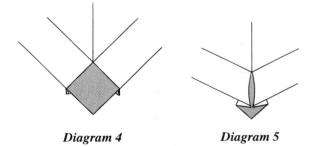

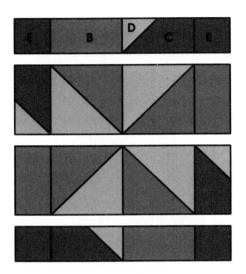

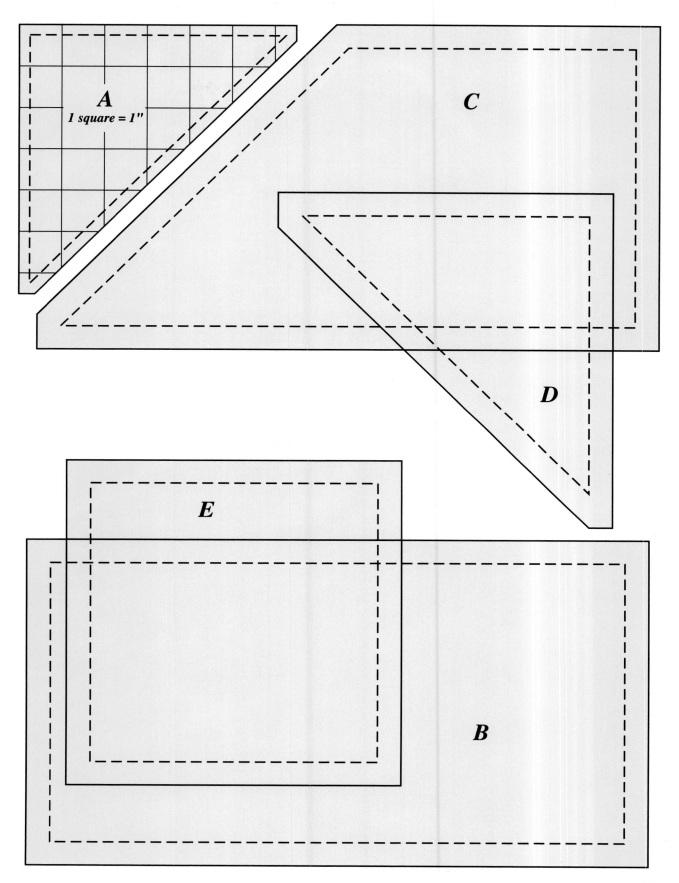

A
1 square = 1"

C

D

E

B

Room by Room, Piece by Piece

Your fingers will trip the light—and dark—fantastic when you piece this striking quilt. The use of a dozen or more prints, all with some degree or another of blue in them, is the element that creates the contrasts. Each block is fashioned from two different prints (four in each light/dark block) to create the overall geometric effect.

Fantasy

Finished size: 48" x 48"

Materials:

3½ yards of dark-blue fabric:
    Two 25" x 50" backing pieces
    5½ yards of 2"-wide bias for binding

2½ yards total of assorted dark-print fabrics:
    96 of Template A
    384 of Template B
    48 of Template C

1¾ yards total of assorted light-print fabrics:
    36 of Template A
    192 of Template B
    48 of Template C

1½ yards of aqua fabric:
    Four 1½" x 50" strips for border

1¾ yards of polyester fleece:
    One 48" x 48" piece

Thread for construction
Quilting thread to match blocks

Directions:

1. **Construct blocks.** Join one light-print B to a different light-print B to make one set (Diagram 1). Repeat to make eight sets. Join the long edges to make one B/B/B/B set. Repeat to make four B/B/B/B sets.

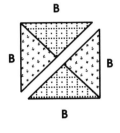

Diagram 1

Using the same two light-prints, join four light-print As (corners), and one different light-print A (center) with the B/B/B/B sets to make three rows (Diagram 2). Join the rows to make one light block. Repeat to make four light blocks. Using two different dark-print fabrics for each block, repeat to make 16 dark blocks.

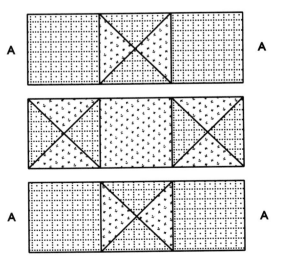

Diagram 2

Join one dark-print C to one light-print C (Diagram 3). Repeat to make three sets.

Join Bs (Diagram 1) to make two light sets and two dark sets. Join sets to As to make one light /dark block (Diagram 4). Repeat to make 16 light/dark blocks.

2. **Construct quilt top.** Join the blocks to make six rows of six blocks, placing the light and dark blocks as noted to create the pattern (see schematic).

3. **Add border.** Join the aqua border strips to the quilt top sides, matching the centers of the long strips to the centers of each edge of the quilt top. Miter the corners.

4. **Mark quilting lines.** Beginning at the upper left corner of the quilt, mark the quilting lines for one quarter of the quilt (Diagram 5). Rotate diagram 90° and mark the quilting lines for the upper right corner. Repeat for the lower right and left corners.

5. **Complete quilt.** Stitch the two backing pieces together along the 50" edges. Layer the quilt back (wrong side up), fleece and quilt top. Baste. Quilt all marked lines with threads that generally match the fabrics. Trim all seam allowances to equal ¼". Bind the edges with the dark-blue border strips. ❖

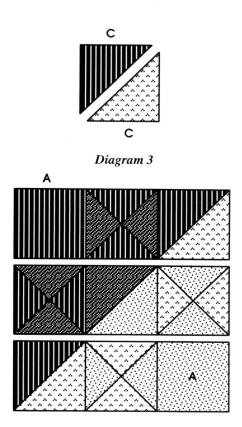

Diagram 3

Diagram 4

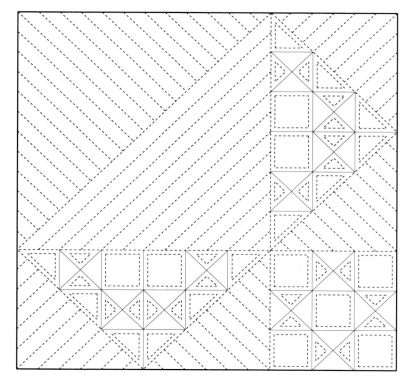

Diagram 5

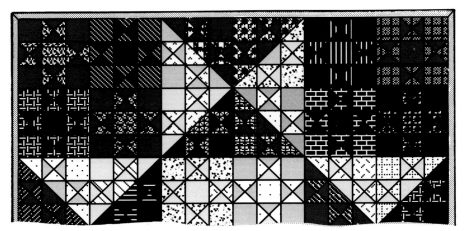

Schematic (upper half of quilt)

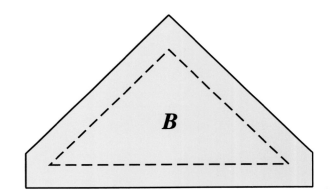

B

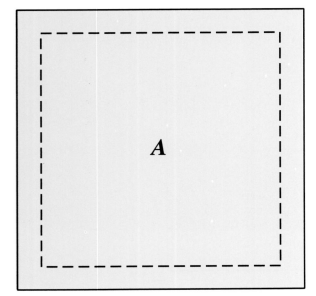

A

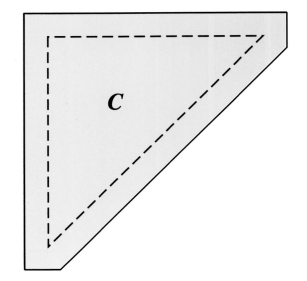

C

Southwestern Wallhanging

Southwestern Wallhanging

Visually inviting, this piece reflects the muted colors of the Southwest in an appealing pattern. It's diminutive yet distinctive—perfect for that small space on the wall just begging to be illuminated by something unique and textured.

Materials:

One yard of light-green fabric:
 One of Template A
 Two of Template F
 One 1" x 9½" strip
 Two 1½" x 3" strips
 Two 1" x 3" strips
 One 10½" x 26" backing piece
 72" of 2"-wide bias strips for binding

⅜ yard of pink fabric:
 Two 3" x 34" strips
 One 1½" x 7½" strip
 One of Template C
 Two of Template F

⅛ yard of aqua fabric:
 One 1¾" x 34" strip
 One 1⅛" x 9½" strip
 One 1½" x 9½" strip
 One 1¼" x 9½" strip

⅛ yard of blue fabric:
 Two 1½" x 9½" strips
 Two of Template B
 Four of Template E
 Two of Template F

⅛ yard of gold fabric:
 One ¾" x 9½" strip
 Two 1" x 9½" strips
 Two of Template F

⅛ yard of mauve fabric:
 One 1½" x 7½" strip
 Three 1" x 9½" strips
 One of Template D

One 9½" x 25" piece of fleece
Pink thread for quilting
Thread for construction

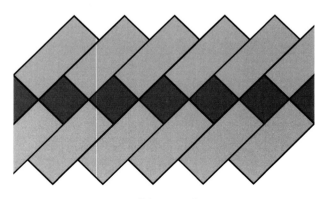

Diagram 1

Directions:

1. **Make diamond sections.** Join the long edges of two 3" x 34" pink strips to both long edges of one 1¾" x 34" aqua strip. Cut into 19 1¾"-wide segments. Join the segments, staggering the pieces, and matching the corners of the aqua pieces, to make one long strip (Diagram 1). Cut strip into three groups of five whole aqua diamonds with a half-diamond on each end (Diagram 1). Cut the diamond strips 1⅞" above and below aqua diamonds to make three 4" x 9½" sections.

2. Construct design section. By hand, set in the pink C to the notch in the light-green A. Join one blue B to each diagonal edge of the green A (Diagram 2). Join two blue Es. Repeat. Set in the mauve D to the E/E set. Repeat on the opposite end of the mauve D.

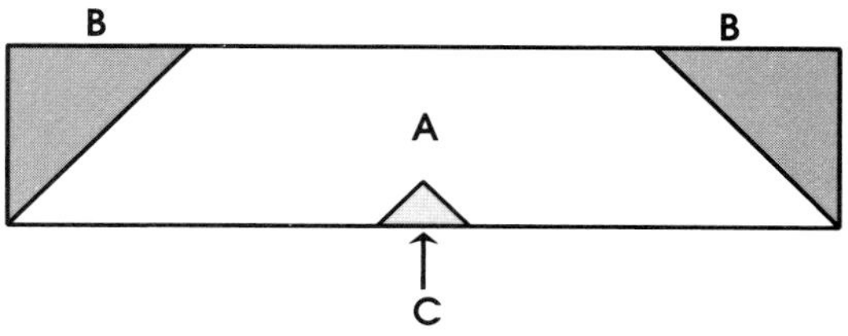

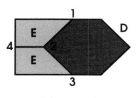

Diagram 3

Using one pink F, one light-green F, one blue F and one gold F, make the square block (Diagram 4). Repeat to make two blocks. Join the blocks to each end of the E/E/D/E/E set.

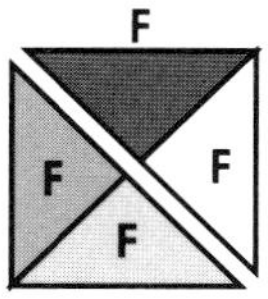

Join the long edges of one mauve and one pink 1½" x 7½" strip. Cut these into 1½"-wide segments. Join the segments together in a row, beginning and ending with a mauve. Discard the extra pink piece. Join the rows to complete the section (Diagram 5).

3. Construct vertical striped section. Join the long edges of two gold and two mauve 1" x 9½" strips, alternating colors. Cut into 3" segments. Join two 1½" x 3" green pieces between the long edges of two gold/ mauve sets. Join 1" x 3" green strips to each end (Diagram 6).

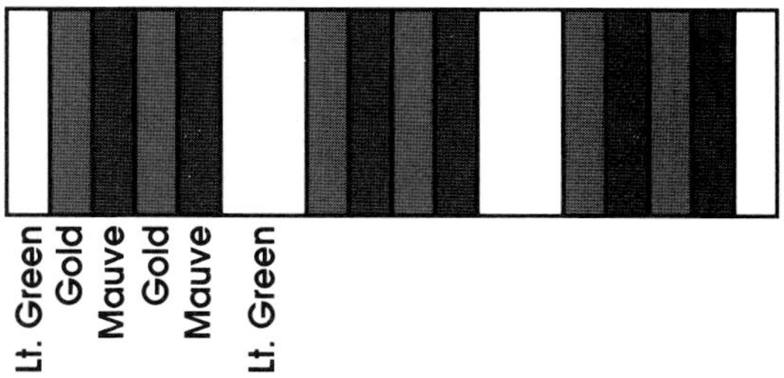

Diagram 7

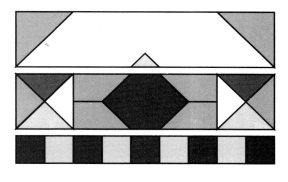

Diagram 2

Diagram 4

Diagram 5

Lt. Green | Gold | Mauve | Gold | Mauve | Lt. Green

Diagram 6

4. Construct wallhanging. Join one 1½" x 9½" blue strip to the top edge of one diamond section. Join one 1⅛" x 9½" aqua strip to the bottom edge of the same diamond section. Then join the ¾" x 9½" gold strip to the bottom edge of the aqua strip. Join with the design section (Diagram 7).

Join the long edges of one green and one mauve 1" x 9½" strip. Join to the top of the second diamond section. Join one 1½" x 9½" blue strip to the bottom edge of the same diamond section. Then join to the vertical striped section (Diagram 8).

Join the 1½" x 9½" aqua strip to the top edge of the third diamond section and the 1¼" x 9½" aqua strip to the bottom edge. Join all sections (see schematic).

5. **Mark quilting lines.** Mark all quilting lines according to the schematic.

6. **Complete wallhanging.** Layer the wallhanging back (wrong side up), fleece and wallhanging top. Baste. Quilt with pink thread on all marked lines. Bind with light-green bias. Miter the corners.

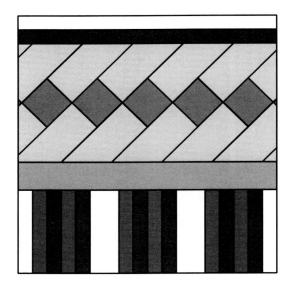

Diagram 8

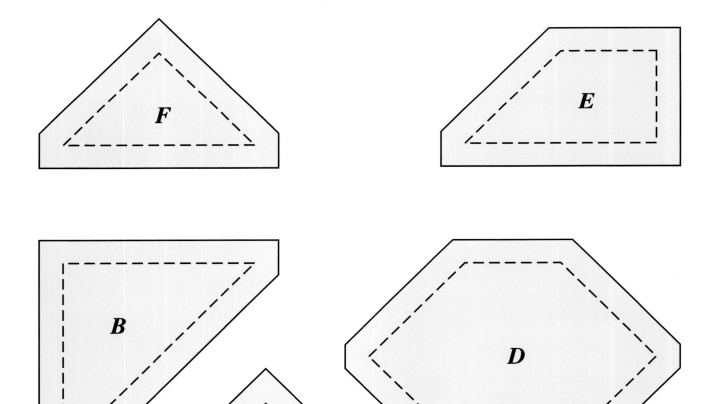

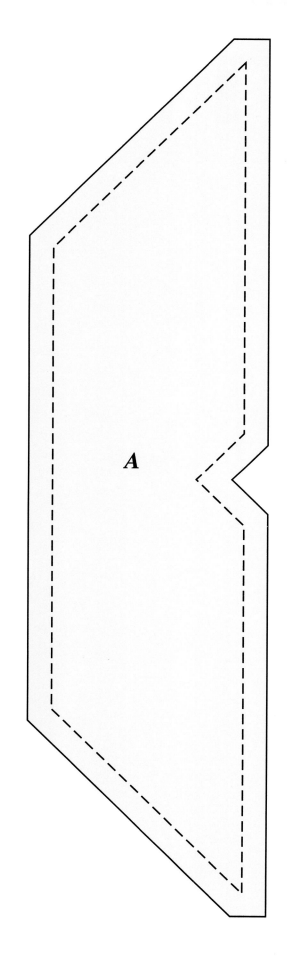

A

Schematic with quilting lines

Tea-Dyed Shower Time

Directions:

1. **Construct checkerboard squares.** Join one long edge of two 1½" x 44" green strips to the long edges of one 1½" x 44" muslin strip. Repeat to make four sets.

   Join one long edge of two 1½" x 44" muslin strips to the long edges of one 1½" x 44" green strips. Repeat to make two sets.

   Cut all five sets into 1½"-wide segments, making 100 green/muslin/green segments and 50 muslin/green/muslin segments.

   Join one long edge of two green/muslin/green segments to the long edge of one muslin/green/muslin strip to make one checkerboard square (Diagram 1). Repeat to make 50 checkerboard squares. Set aside.

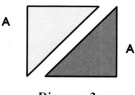

Diagram 1

2. **Construct design blocks.** Join one muslin A to one green A on the long edge (Diagram 2). Repeat to make 120 sets. Set aside.

Diagram 2

Join one long edge of two 1½" x 44" green strips to the long edges of one 1½" x 44" muslin strip. Repeat to make 10 sets. Cut the sets into 3½"-wide segments, making 120 (Diagram 3).

Diagram 3

Spruce up your shower area with this clever curtain. We used an old quilt pattern—the monkey wrench—and then aged it to perfection with a tea-dying technique.

Finished Size: 77" x 65"

Materials:

12 yards of muslin:
    120 of Template A
    49 3½" x 9½" sashing pieces
    28 1½" x 44" strips
    13 6½" x 11" loop pieces
    9 yards of 3"-wide bias for binding
    Two 2½" x 57½" border pieces
    Two 2½" x 73½" border pieces
    Two 3¾" x 65½" border pieces
    Two 3¾" x 84" border pieces
    Two 44" x 74" backing pieces

3 yards of green fabric:
    120 of Template A
    40 1½" x 44" strips

Polyester fleece:
    Two 44" x 72" pieces

Cream thread for quilting
Six to eight large tea bags

Join four A/A sets, one checkerboard square and four
3½"-wide segments to make three rows (Diagram 4).
Join the rows to make one design block. Repeat to
make 30 design blocks.

3. **Piece center.** Join six design blocks to the long edges
of five 3½" x 9½" muslin sashing pieces to make Rows
1, 3, 5, 7 and 9 (Diagram 5).

Join the short edges of six 3½" x 9½" muslin sashing
pieces to five checkerboard squares to make Rows 2, 4,
6 and 8 (Diagram 6). Join the rows to make the center
of the shower curtain (see schematic).

Diagram 4

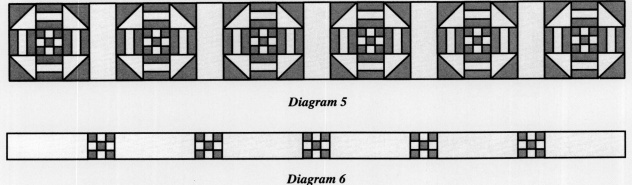

Diagram 5

Diagram 6

4. **Add border.** Stitch one 2½" x 57½" muslin strip to
each side edge of center section. Stitch one 2½" x
73½" strip to top and bottom edges of center section.

Stitch one 1½" x 44" green strip to the long edge of one
1½" x 44" muslin strip. Repeat to make 10 sets. Cut
into 1½"-wide segments. Join the segments to make
two 2½" x 61½" strips, alternating colors. Stitch one
checkerboard strip to each side edge of the shower
curtain. Join remaining segments to make two 2½" x
77½"strips. Stitch one checkerboard strip to the top and
bottom edges of shower curtain.

Stitch one 3¾" x 65½" muslin strip to each side edge.
Then stitch one 3¾" x 84" muslin strip to the top and
bottom edges.

5. **Layer shower curtain.** Stitch the two backing pieces
together along the 74" edge. Layer the backing (wrong
side up), fleece and shower curtain top. Baste.

Quilt-in-the-ditch all four edges of the checkerboard
center in each block. Then stitch-in-the-ditch of all
sashing and checkerboard post pieces.

6. **Bind shower curtain.** Fold the bias to measure 1½"
wide. Stitch to the front of the shower curtain, aligning
the raw edges and using ½" seam allowances.

Fold one shower curtain tab to measure 3¼" wide.
Stitch the long edge. Turn. Repeat to make 13 tabs.
Fold to make 5½"-deep loops. Pin the raw ends
together. Pin to the back top edge of the shower curtain
with all raw edges aligned. Stitch the tabs in place on
the stitching line of the bias binding.

Fold the binding to the wrong side and slipstitch. Fold
the tabs up and topstitch the tabs to the outside edge of
the bias binding.

7. **Tea-dye shower curtain.** Fill washer for small load
with hot water. Add six to eight large tea bags (equiva-
lent to three individual-serving size bags). Add shower
curtain. Allow the shower curtain to agitate until the
desired darkness is achieved. Dry the shower curtain in
dryer at setting appropriate for cotton. (Fabric will dry
lighter than it appears when wet. The heat sets the
color. To air-dry the shower curtain can result in
streaks or "water marks.")

Schematic (upper left corner)

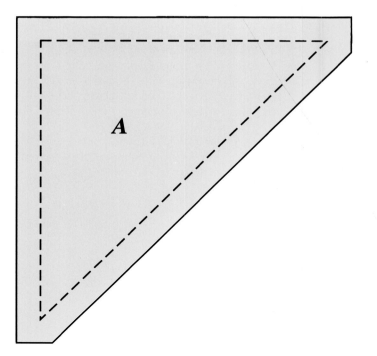

A

Busy Holidays

Stocking

Finished size: 17" tall

Materials:

One package of 12 coordinating solid colored fabrics in 18" x 22" pieces*
Cut into strips in widths varying from ½" to 1¼". Begin with three strips of each color of fabric, including green and turquoise.

½ yard of green fabric:
One STOCKING for back
60" of 1¼"-wide bias
One 1" x 4" piece for loop

½ yard of turquoise fabric:
Two STOCKINGs for lining

½ yard of flannel:
One STOCKING

Six ⅜"-wide pearl buttons
Thread for construction
1¾ yards of small cording

*Available from:
Quilts and Other Comforts
6700 W. 44th Avenue
Wheatridge, CO 80033
Item #FP35

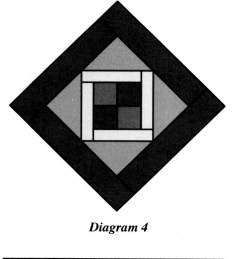

Buttons, checkerboards, log cabin quilting, squares and stripes, all in bright and bold colors—this holiday set has it all!

Directions:

1. **Piece pattern designs.** Construct four or more pieced patterns before beginning (Diagrams 1-5). Most can be made from the strips already cut. For example, to make the checkerboard, join the long edges of two contrasting strips. If the strips are 1" wide, cut 1"-wide sets. Join the sets to make a checkerboard strip. To make the rainbow strip (see photo), join the long edges of 1"-wide strips in seven colors. Then cut into 1" sets and join. Another pattern can be made by joining five or six strips of random widths and colors. Use this piece as one piece of fabric to fill some areas. See Log Cabin Piecing in the General Instructions.

Diagram 1

Diagram 2

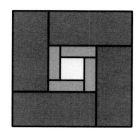

Diagram 3

Diagram 4

Diagram 5

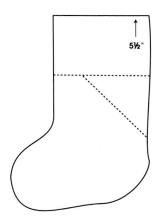

5½"

Diagram 6

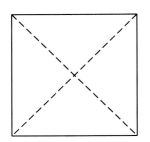

Diagram 7

2. **Make stocking front.** On the flannel stocking, mark a horizontal guideline 5½ " below and parallel to the top edge of the stocking. Then mark one 45-degree angle at any point below the intersection (Diagram 6). All seams will be parallel to or at a 45-degree angle to these lines. Mark additional guidelines as needed.

Place the first strip right side up and parallel to the diagonal guideline; pin. Place the second strip right side down on top of and matching one edge of the first strip; stitch. Unfold and press. Repeat, working in both directions from the first strip. Then piece the top of the stocking, keeping all seams parallel to the horizontal line and each other. Continue to piece the stocking front, integrating sets as desired.

3. **Construct stocking.** Make 60" of corded piping using the green bias. Stitch to the sides and the bottom of the stocking front. Stitch the stocking front and back with the right sides together, sewing on the stitching line of the piping. Turn. Cut 10 4" x 4" pieces for the cuff, all of the same color. Fold into triangles (Diagram 7). Pin to the top edge of the stocking, spacing evenly (see photo). Baste. Stitch the piping over the folded triangles around the top edge of the stocking. Add the buttons as desired (see photo). Fold a 1" x 4" piece to measure ½" wide. Stitch along the long edge. Turn. Topstitch the edges. Fold to make a 2" loop. Pin the raw ends of the loop to the right side seam. Stitch the two lining pieces together, leaving an opening in the side seam above the heel; do not turn. Slide the lining over the stocking, matching the side seams at the top edge. Stitch on the stitching line of the piping. Turn through the opening in the lining, Slipstitch the opening closed. Fold the lining inside the stocking.

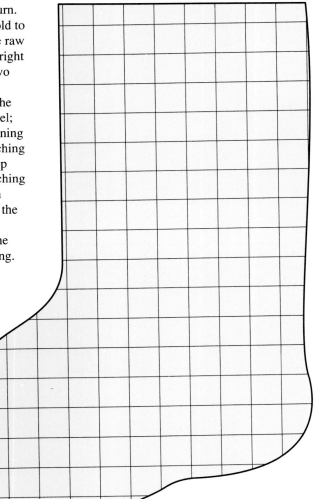

STOCKING

1 square = 1"
Final size = 17" tall

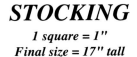

Directions:

1. **Piece pattern designs.** Construct four to six pieced patterns for each panel before beginning; see Step 1 of the stocking. Also make folded triangles in two or three dominant colors; see Step 3 of the stocking.

2. **Piece panels.** On a flannel SKIRT panel, mark a line at any angle. Plan the piecing patterns in relation to the marked line, checking parallel and right angle seams frequently. Mark additional guidelines as needed.

   Place the first strip right side up and parallel to the guideline. Place the second strip right side down on top of and matching one edge of the first strip; stitch. Unfold and press. Repeat the procedure, working in both directions from the first strip. Continue to piece each panel, integrating the sets as desired. Larger, less detailed pieces may be used near the narrow end of the panels as they are less likely to show.

3. **Construct tree skirt.** Place the pattern over each pieced panel; cut out. Stitch the panels together on the sides. Make 6 yards of piping. Stitch to the outside edge and the "neck" edge.

   Stitch the green pieces for the backing together on the long edges. Fold into quarters and mark 3" and 33" from the center. Cut on the marks. Stitch the outside and the center back edges of the tree skirt top and back with the right sides together. Turn. Slipstitch the "neck" closed. Add the buttons as desired, then attach the hook-and-eye sets to the center back edges. ❖

Tree Skirt

Finished Size: Approximately 65 " in diameter

Materials:

Three packages of coordinating fabrics (see stocking materials):
   Cut into strips in widths ranging from ¼" increments from ½" to 2". Begin with 12-15 strips of each color, including green. Cut more as needed.

5½ yards of green fabric:
   One 45" x 66" backing piece
   One 22" x 66" backing piece
   6 yards of 1½"-wide bias for binding

3 yards of flannel:
   Seven SKIRTs, adding 1" to outside edges of pattern

Assorted buttons in primary colors
Thread for construction
6 yards of small cording
Four large hook-and-eye sets

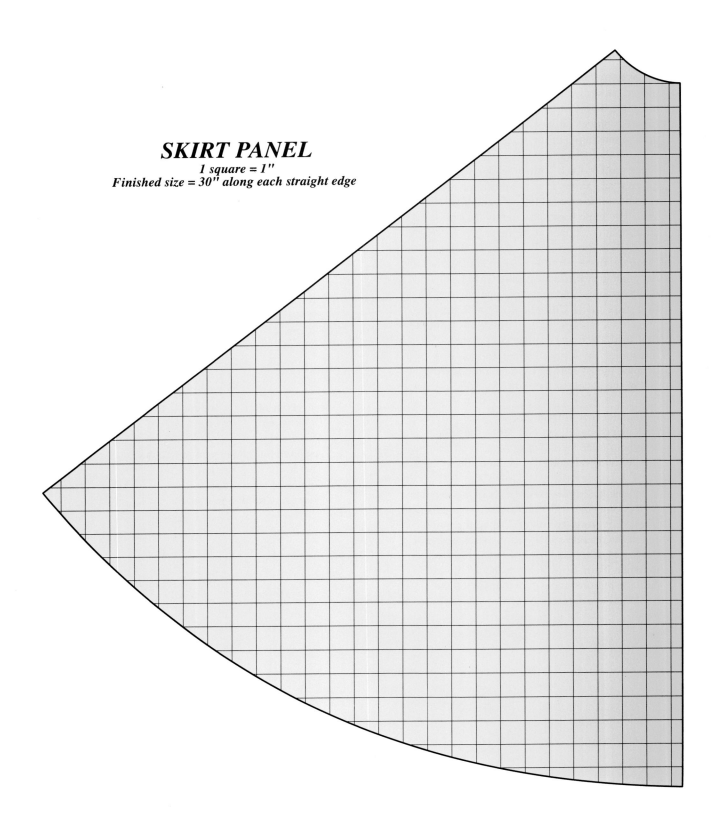

SKIRT PANEL
1 square = 1"
Finished size = 30" along each straight edge

Checkerboard Rainbow

Quilt this comfortable coverlet in a palette of colors; then fold it into the built-in pocket, and voila—it's a pillow!

Finished size: 55" x 73"

Materials:

2¾ yards of white fabric:
    Two 38" x 59" backing pieces
    One 15" x 18" pocket backing piece
    22 2" x 44" strips
    230 of Template A

¾ yard of blue fabric:
    105 of Template A

¾ yard of pink fabric:
    105 of Template A

⅛ yard each of ten to 12 assorted colors:
    22 2" x 44" strips

½ yard of light-green fabric:
    One 15" x 18" pocket backing piece
    7¼ yards of 2"-wide bias for binding

One 57" x 75" piece of batting

Directions:

1. **Make diamond blocks.** Join one white A to one blue A (Diagram 1). Repeat to make 105 blue A/A sets.

Diagram 1

Join one white A to one pink A. Repeat to make 105 pink A/A sets. Join the sets to make blocks, alternating the colors (Diagram 2). Make 47 blocks. Also make 20 half-blocks. (One pink A/A set and one blue A/A set will remain.)

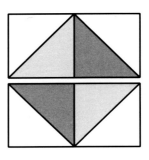

Diagram 2

2. **Make square blocks.** Join the long edges of one white 2" x 44" strip and one colored 2" x 44" strip. Cut this strip into 2"-wide segments. Repeat, matching all of the strips in white/colored pairs. Then cut all of the strips into segments, making 456. Join the segments, combining the colors at random (Diagrams 3 and 4). Make 47 blocks. Also make 20 half-blocks.

Diagram 3

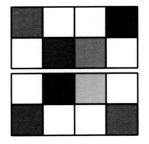

Diagram 4

3. Assemble quilt top. Join the half-blocks and the remaining sets to make Rows 1 and 13 (Diagram 5). Set these aside.

To make Rows 2 through 12, use one diamond half-block, one square half-block, four diamond blocks and four square blocks (Diagram 6).

Row 1

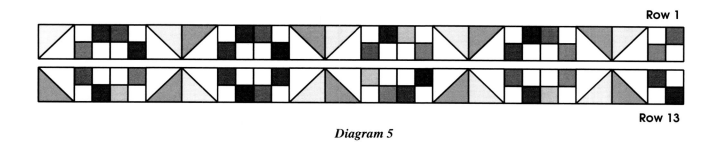

Row 13

Diagram 5

Rows 2-12

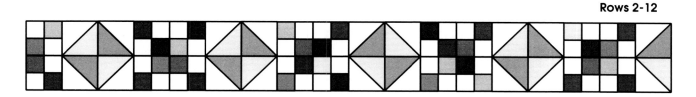

Diagram 6

Diagram 7

Join the rows, placing the pattern and the square blocks so that the colors are totally random (see schematic). Assemble the remaining pieces for the pocket (Diagram 7).

Diagram 8

4. **Complete quilt.** Join the long edges of the two 38" x 59" backing pieces. Layer the backing (wrong side up), the batting and the quilt top. Baste. Repeat with the white pocket backing, the batting and the pocket piece. Quilt all of both pieces by machine (Diagram 8).

5. **Attach pocket.** Place the pocket and the green pocket backing piece with the right sides together. Stitch both sides and the top edge. Clip the corners. Turn. On the back of the quilt, mark the center of one edge. Also mark the center of the open bottom edge of the pocket. Placing the right side of the pocket against the back of the quilt and matching the centers, baste the pocket to the quilt. Topstitch the sides of the pocket securely.

6. **Complete quilt.** Bind the quilt with the green bias, mitering the corners and securing the bottom edge of the pocket.

To fold the quilt into the pocket, fold the outside edges over the center (Diagram 9). Then fold into fourths and turn the pocket wrong side out (Diagram 10). ❖

Diagram 9

Diagram 10

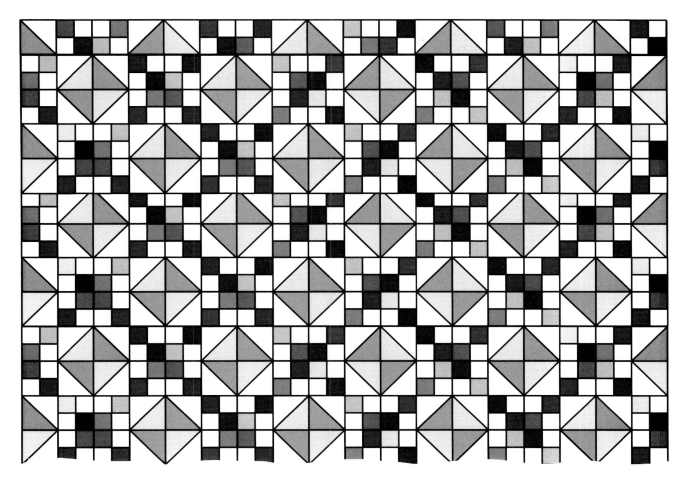

Schematic (upper half)

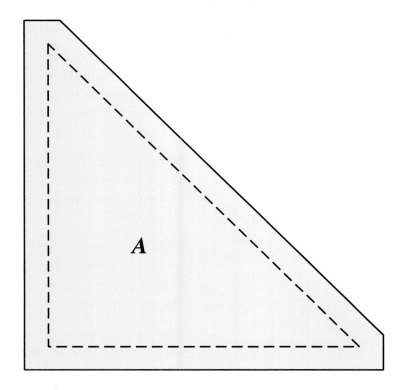

A

General Instructions

Today's quilter has dozens of beautiful quilting books from which to select. Each is as different as the authors themselves. Some focus on color while others may choose traditional, step-by-step construction details, the how-tos of quilting geometry, or the spirit and history of quilts.

If you are a beginner, inquire at your local quilt store or library about books that cover basic techniques. You can also sign up for quilt classes, keeping in mind that no teacher is absolutely the last word on this art form. If you are an experienced quilter, look for books that feature shortcuts or new tools. There is always a new trick for you to learn.

Once you have selected your project from this book, read through the directions and the general instructions. You are now ready to begin. We wish you success!

Supplies needed

Many of the projects in this book require the following:

Dressmakers' pen, chalk or a #2 lead pencil
Clear quilters' ruler with a 45° angle marked
Dressmakers' scissors
Rotary cutter and mat
Quilting needles

Preliminary instructions

Because many of the projects in *Living With Quilts* are advanced, an explanation of some basic quilting techniques will be defined here for reference.

Fabric requirements are based upon 44"/45"-wide selections. Wash, dry and press the fabrics prior to making the quilt. Shrinkage varies among fabrics. Trim all of the selvage; don't use it in any of the pieces.

Pattern templates and measurements for pieces and strips include ¼" seam allowances, except where noted. When working with small pieces, the seam allowances may touch or overlap; if so, trim them to ⅛".

Measurements for backing pieces and border strips are cut larger than the finished size to allow for some inevitable shifting between the layers.

Each fabric is identified to match those used in the photographed models. The information is intended as a guide, not to confine you. Experiment with different colors and textures.

The finished size of a project is based upon measurements before any quilting is done.

Making templates

Using vinyl, cardboard, plastic or sandpaper, make your templates (patterns). The size and number of each template needed will determine which product to use. Be sure and label each template.

Enlarging patterns

Choose a sheet of paper that is large enough to accommodate the finished size of the pattern. Mark grid lines 1" apart to fill the paper. Begin marking dots on 1" grid lines where the reduced pattern intersects the corresponding grid line. Connect the dots.

Available in fabric stores is a pattern-enlarging product (Pattern Pelon ™) that has small dots at 1" intervals. Graph paper can also be used to eliminate the tedious process of hand drawing grid lines.

Cutting fabrics

The rule-of-thumb for quilting is to cut all pieces before beginning to sew. However, with the more complex quilts in this book, the cutting instructions are sometimes given one block at a time to avoid confusing pieces which are similar. Either way, be sure to have plenty of fabric on hand in the event of a mistake. Identify and store pieces in boxes or envelopes—anything that will keep an unruly piece in a safe place.

Whenever possible, speed-quilting techniques have been incorporated into the instructions. This explains what may seem like an error in the cutting instructions for some quilts.

Begin cutting the largest pieces first, tracing all patterns onto the wrong side of the fabric before cutting. Generally, one or more of the straight sides of the template will follow the grain line.

Piecing quilt top

The following pertains to piecing a quilt top in general terms. Each quilt in this book is different; therefore, choose the information that best suits each individual project. The techniques of **setting-in**, **strip piecing** and **segments** are also detailed.

Piecing a quilt by hand works best for a design with small pieces. Work from precisely marked ¼" seam lines. Place the pieces with right sides together and sew the seams through the marked lines. Begin and end each stitch at the seam line (not the edge of the fabric), with two or three backstitches.

With machine-pieced work, if the presser foot is ¼"-wide, the edge of the fabric can be aligned with its edge, resulting in a precise seam line.

Look for places to **chain piece**; it is an easy way to progress to completion of the quilt top. To chain piece, sew the seam to join two pieces. Then, without removing the piece from the sewing mancine or lifting the presser foot, start sewing the next two pieces together. Sew all seams through to the cut edge unless you are inserting a piece at an angle.

Do all **pressing** with a dry iron. Press all seams to one side, usually toward the darker fabrics. Blocks should be square, measuring the same size. If problems occur with individual blocks, remove a few stitches and repair. Press everything—blocks, sashing and borders—before completing assembly.

Many quilts are constructed in rows. Sew the blocks together to create rows, adding sashing if called for. Then, sew the rows together to complete the quilt top. When setting blocks and rows together, avoid stretching them as you sew.

The process of **setting-in** is used to sew a piece into an angle. The pieces are joined exactly at the areas indicated (Diagram 1).

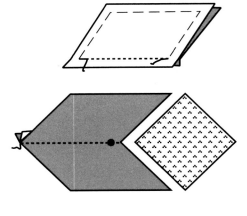

Diagram 1

When sewing the pieces that form the angle, end the stitching ¼" from the edge; backstitch or knot the end. When machine stitching, pin one angle piece to one edge of the patch with right sides together, matching corners. Stitch from the corner to the end of the seam in the direction of the arrow (Diagram 2); backstitch.

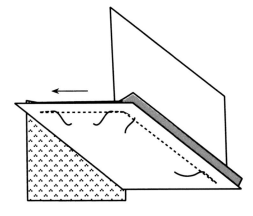

Diagram 2

One of the quickest ways to create striking geometrical designs is with the use of **strip piecing** and **segments**. Simply sew strips of fabric together on the long edges. Then cut the pieced strips into segments, adding ½" for the seam allowance (Diagram 3).

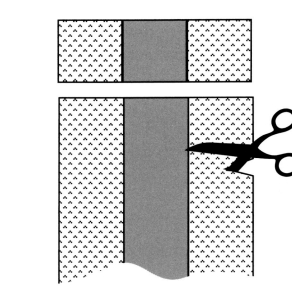

Diagram 3

For example, if the desired finished design is 1"-wide, cut the pieced strips into 1½" segments. Press, then re-sew the segments together into the desired design.

When making a checkerboard, it is necessary to add or remove a block on alternating rows. The easiest way, although some fabric is wasted, is to make extra segmemts and remove the stitching of extra blocks.

Quilting

Quilting not only strengthens a piece but turns an ordinary quilt into a masterpiece.

To hand quilt, use a small needle. Quilting thread is waxed and therefore stronger than sewing thread, but sewing thread can be used, especially if a special color is needed. Begin quilting from the center.

Log Cabin piecing

Log Cabin piecing is the technique used to make a block using contrasting strips for the "logs" and a center square for the "chimney". Stitch the strips clockwise on the center square (turning the block counterclockwise) (Diagrams 4 and 5). Trim the excess fabric from each consecutive strip. Continue in this order until the block is completed.

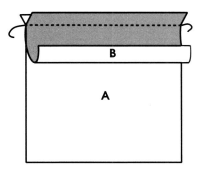

Diagram 4

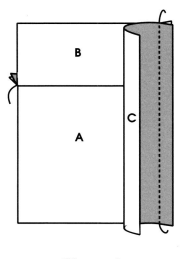

Diagram 5

Layering

For large, bulky projects, secure all layers together with safety pins. Then, baste a loose running stitch from the center out, first dividing the quilt into quarters, then eighths. For small, lightweight pieces, safety pins are all that are needed.

Crazy quilting

Crazy quilting is a piecing technique using small, irregularly shaped pieces of fabric on a muslin (or other fabric) background. Beginning in one corner, pin the irregular shapes, one at a time, to the background fabric, turning the raw edges under and overlapping each consecutive piece over the previous one; blindstitch (Diagram 6). Continue in this fashion until the entire background is covered.

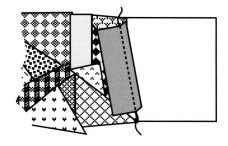

Diagram 6

Applique

Applique adds detail and curved lines that are not available in pieced designs. In most cases, the seam allowances will be turned under, but if the appliqued pieces overlap, leave the seam allowances flat. Clip the seam allowances of inside curved edges. Cut the smaller "V"-shaped pieces on the outside corners to reduce bulk.

Fold the seam allowances to the wrong side; press and/or baste. Place the design piece right side up on the right side of the fabric and slipstitch to the quilt top with close, small stitches, using matching thread. A decorative stitch may be added to the edge.

Borders

Borders "frame" the quilt. The simplest borders are strips that are first pinned to two opposite edges. Then, two more strips are joined to the remaining sides and extend beyond the ends of the first two strips.

Mitered borders have diagonal seams in each corner. To miter the corner, center the border strip on each side. Pin, baste and sew strips to—but not through—the seam line; backstitch at each end. Repeat the process on all four sides. Stitching lines should meet exactly at each corner. Fold two adjacent border pieces together at each corner. Mark, then sew a 45° angle. Trim the seam allowances to ¼" (Diagram 7).

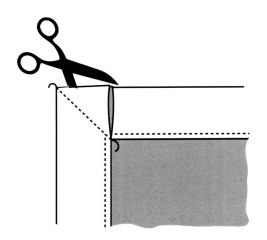

Diagram 7

When the quilt border has more than one parallel strip of fabric, regardless of the width, it is easier to join all the strips together and miter them all at once.

Binding

Once the quilting is complete, trim the backing and batting to match the quilt top. A bias binding is the most common way to cover raw edges. For a wall hanging or small piece that will not receive much wear, a single-layer bias binding is adequate. Stitch the right side of the binding and quilt top together, matching raw edges. Fold the binding to the wrong side of the quilt, covering the raw edge and

folding under ¼". Slipstitch the folded edge to the quilt back (Diagram 8).

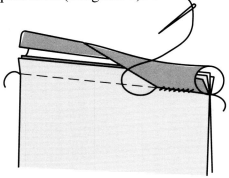

Diagram 8

For a bed quilt or other piece that requires a stronger binding, a double-layer bias binding is best. Cut the bias twice as wide as the single binding minus ½". Fold the binding in half lengthwise; press. With the folded edge of binding facing the center of the quilt, and with the raw edges of the binding matching the raw edges of the quilt, slipstitch the binding to the quilt top. Fold the binding over the raw edge of the quilt and slipstitch the folded edge to the backing.

To miter the corners of a bias binding, stitch the binding to the quilt top, stopping ¼" from each corner; backstitch. Fold the bias on the corners at a right angle. Resume stitching with a backstitch ¼" from the corner. Then, when slipstitching the binding to the back, fold the bias with a mitered corner on both sides.

Finishing touch

Signing and dating your masterpiece not only enhances its meaning but adds to its value for future generations. One way to do this is to write your name and date on a scrap of washed fabric and slipstitch it to the back of the quilt. Another is to embroider the information onto muslin. If you have had experience cross-stitching, you might cross-stitch or backstitch your name and date on Aida 18 or a similar fabric and slipstitch it to the back of the quilt. ◈

Glossary

APPLIQUE: A design made by cutting shapes from one or more fabrics and applying them by hand or machine to another piece of fabric. (See General Instructions.)

BACKING: The fabric that forms the bottom or back layer of the quilt.

BACKSTITCH: Very short stitches used in hand piecing at the beginning or end of a line of stitching to secure the threads.

BASTING STITCHES: Temporary stitches used to hold the fabric in place while quilting.

BATTING (sometimes called batt): The filler or middle part that goes between the quilt top and the backing. It provides thickness and warmth to the quilt. Most batting is a polyester product and should be bonded. Some projects use cotton flannel.

BIAS: The diagonal of a woven fabric in which a true 45° angle is formed. The bias has the greatest amount of stretch. A line diagonal to the greater elasticity than fabric cut on the lengthwise or crosswise grain.

BINDING: A narrow strip of fabric used to enclose the raw outer edges of the quilt top, batting and backing. It can be cut on either the straight grain or the bias. (See General Instructions for ways to attach binding.)

BLOCK: A unit of patchwork, usually in the form of a square, repeated to construct an entire quilt top.

BORDER: Plain, pieced, or appliqued band(s) of fabric surrounding the central section of the quilt top. (See General Instructions for ways to attach borders.)

CHAIN PIECING: An easy way to speed up machine piecing, without removing the sewn piece from the sewing machine before sewing the next two pieces together.

CORDED PIPING: Cording covered with a fabric bias strip.

CRAZY QUILTING: A form of patchwork in which random shapes of fabric are stitched to a foundation block. Embroidery stitches may accent the seams.

ECHO-QUILT: To quilt in concentric rows parallel to a seam or the edge of an appliqued piece.

ENLARGING A PATTERN: The process of making a small pattern larger by using grid lined paper or Pattern Pellon ™ (See "Enlarging Patterns" in General Instructions).

GRAIN: The lengthwise and crosswise threads of a woven fabric used in its construction.

GRID: Squares of a uniform size such as those used in the quilted pattern of a quilt.

HAND QUILTING: Small running stitches which hold the three layers of the quilt together, either following a design which has been marked on the quilt top or following the outline of a pieced or appliqued block.

IN-THE-DITCH: Quilting done as close as possible to the seam. May be used on seams which join blocks or on a foundation very close to an appliqued design.

LAYERING: The process of placing the three layers of the quilt together.

LOFT: The springiness or fluffiness of a fiber.

LOG CABIN PIECING: A quilting technique in which each block consists of a center square (the "chimney") with strips stitched around it (the "logs"). (See General Instructions.)

MIRROR-IMAGE: Quilt pieces cut the same size and shape but reversed as if seen in a mirror.

MITER: Joining vertical and horizontal strips of fabric at a 45° angle to form a 90° angle. (See "Borders" in General Instructions.)

PATTERN: Any design of a quilt usually repeated several times on the quilt top. Sometimes referred to as "design."

PIECING/PIECED BLOCK: Pieces of cut fabric sewn together to produce a pattern, usually in the form of a block.

QUILTING/QUILTING STITCHES: Stitches used to secure the three layers of the quilt together. The quilting can be done either by hand or machine.

QUILT TOP: The top layer of the quilt. It can be pieced, appliqued or a combination of the two.

ROTARY CUTTER: An advantage modern quilters have is the use of this tool for cutting fabric. The cutter is placed flush against a sturdy acrylic ruler and with a sharp round blade, as many as six layers of fabric can be cut. This tool is used on a cutting mat, some of which have a 1" grid and 45° angles marked on them.

RUNNING STITCH: A simple up-and-down stitch used for hand piecing.

SAMPLER QUILT: A pieced and/or appliqued quilt composed of many different block designs.

SASHING: The strip of fabric used between blocks to separate and set them together.

SCRAP: Any 12" x 12" or smaller piece or pieces of fabric.

SEAM: The stitched junction of two pieces of fabric, right sides together, with a ¼" seam allowance. Can be done either by hand or machine.

SEAM ALLOWANCE: The distance between the cut edge of the fabric and the stitching line.

SEGMENTS/STRIP PIECING: Fabrics pieced together that look as if each piece were joined separately, but were actually cut from pieced strips. (See "Piecing" in General Instructions.)

SETTING-IN: Sewing one fabric piece into the angle of another. (See "Piecing" in General Instructions.)

SLIPSTITCH: A small, almost invisible stitch used to secure a folded edge to a flat surface.

STENCILLING: A painting technique that utilizes Mylar, vinyl or cardboard templates, acrylic paints and blunt-end brushes.

TEMPLATE: An individual model of a part of a pattern block made from cardboard, plastic, sandpaper or vinyl. ◆

INDEX

All of us at Meredith® Press are dedicated to offering you, our customer, the best books we can create. We are particularly concerned that all of the instructions for making projects are clear and accurate. Please address your correspondence to: Customer Service Department, Meredith® Press, Meredith Corporation, 150 East 52nd Street, New York, NY 10022

If you are interested in any other titles from The Vanessa-Ann Collection or Meredith Books, please write to Meredith Books, P.O. Box 10670, Des Moines, IA 50336, or call 1-800-678-2665.

For information on how you can have *Better Homes and Gardens* delivered to your door, write to: Mr. Robert Austin, P.O. Box 4536, Des Moines, IA 50336